MAKING INEQUALITY

The Hidden Curriculum of High School Tracking

JAMES E. ROSENBAUM

A WILEY-INTERSCIENCE PUBLICATION
JOHN WILEY & SONS, New York • London • Sydney • Toronto

To my mother
Dorothy B. Rosenbaum

and my father
Irving Rosenbaum, Jr.

Copyright © 1976 by John Wiley & Sons, Inc.

All rights reserved. Published simultaneously in Canada.

No part of this book may be reproduced by any means, nor transmitted, nor translated into a machine language without the written permission of the publisher.

Library of Congress Cataloging in Publication Data
Rosenbaum, James E.   1943–
    Making inequality.

    "A Wiley-Interscience publication."
    Bibliography: p.
    Includes index.
    1. High schools—Administration.   2. Ability grouping in education.   3. High school students—Attitudes.   I.   Title.
    LB2822.R67   373.1'2'54   76–2008

ISBN 0–471–73605–8

Printed in the United States of America

10 9 8 7 6 5 4 3 2 1

Foreword

The interest of social scientists, school professionals, policymakers, and the public in the school's role as a perpetuator or ameliorator of the class system has increased steadily over the past generation. Such landmark studies as Warner, Havighurst, and Loeb's *Who Shall Be Educated?* and Hollingshead's *Elmtown's Youth* have been followed recently by the more broadly based and methodologically sophisticated Coleman report and the work of Jencks et al.

It is no wonder that more and more attention is paid to the role of the schools in modern society, since they consume an ever-increasing portion of the economy's product. In 1930 United States school expenditures were 3.1% of the gross national product. In 1974 it was more than double that amount. By then 7.4% of the vastly greater gross national product was devoted to public and private education. Schooling is not solely an American fixation; in post World War II Europe there has been a similar rapid growth in the proportion of the national product devoted to education. Social science research of all kinds—economic, sociological, psychological, anthropological, historical—is needed to help us understand what we are doing, what we think we are accomplishing, and what, in fact, is being accomplished.

Sociologists have quite naturally been drawn to studying the school's relationship to society's stratification system. On the one hand, schools sort people into more or less accomplished groups. On the other hand, that sorting has been believed to moderate the ascriptive forces in the stratification system. To understand fully what the schools actually do in these respects, investigators do sample surveys, such as the Coleman report, and examine intensively interpersonal relationships within particular school systems.

The national sample survey studies give us an opportunity to understand something of the distribution of school characteristics and their gross relationships to various kinds of outcome. But they shed relatively little light on the day-to-day processes by which schools accomplish their results. Intensive observational surveys that concern themselves with what goes on in classrooms between teachers and pupils and, ideally, between teachers and teachers and teachers and administrators can tell us a great deal about how school life is actually lived. By their very nature, however, such studies are less likely to probe the long-term effect of these institutionalized processes on the actors in schools. James Rosenbaum's study strikes a nice balance between a focus on effects and a focus on process. As a case study it describes in detail the effects of one school's operation, rather than those of the school as an institution in the whole society. The use of several methods, both of data collection and of analysis, allows Rosenbaum to present a well-rounded picture of how one particular aspect of the school as an institution, that of tracking, operates on and affects the school experience. *Making Inequality* sets its school in the context of a particular community and relates its operations to its role in the worlds of the economy, of work, of the government, and of the family.

One learns, not surprisingly, that much of what goes on in this school suggests that it is responsive first to the professional and bureaucratic imperatives of itself as an institution, second to those of the larger society, and only then to the needs and desires of the family and its students.

In all of this the school reflects the patterns of inequality in the society and plays an important role in establishing and projecting into the future the identities of working-class children in this school. That the community involved is a relatively homogeneous working-class community provides a kind of useful control for the study of tracking. In this case tracking does not serve the function of sorting the students out into their parents' social status groups. In the metropolitan area that is done quite effectively through residential segregation and the institution of the neighborhood school. Instead, it is as if some social dynamic stimulates the school to sort the students simply because they are there. One could find almost equally homogeneous upper-middle-class schools that also sort their students into tracks. An interesting companion study would analyze the history and current institutional rationale of tracking as a professional ideology.

In a highly systematic and very careful way Rosenbaum shows us effects of the tracking process on the students' intellectual performance and their view of themselves. We cannot yet know how long these effects persist in the children's lives, but it is certainly true that at an important time of their lives too many of these students have their intellectual inferiority communicated to them as authoritatively as a school can manage. Thus the school serves to liberate very, very few of these working-class children from their class background, not just in the sense of helping only a few of them to be socially mobile but in the more basic sense of giving few of them a level of self-confidence that would strengthen their ability to operate in a complex world in which most of them will spend their lives rather low on the totem pole. Instead, the students turn, as many studies of "youth culture" have documented, to their peers for the ability to resist the insults and injuries of class, much as they will turn later to their immediate families and their adult peers. However, many studies of working-class life and culture indicate that these defenses against their position of relative disadvantage, sometimes even of insecure affluence, are not sufficient to prevent a sense of depression and nervous alienation from affecting many working-class people.

Many school reformers have aspired to producing a school system that enables the growing child to free himself somewhat from the pressures of his place in society. Perhaps it does, compared to no schooling at all. But it is clear that the professionalism of education has institutionalized many practices that interfere with the student's self-realization and mastery of his or her world, and of these institutionalized practices none is so blatant as tracking.

LEE RAINWATER

March 1976

Preface

Social equality is one of our nation's fundamental ideals. Contemporary investigations of educational equality, including the Coleman Report and Jencks's book *Inequality,* have been interpreted to say that schools cannot effect the goal of social equality. But that is not what Jencks concludes. Although he finds that differences between schools do not have effects, he discovers that the selection systems within schools do have a significant effect on equality. This conclusion gives us reason for hope, not only because it tells us that something makes a difference, but also because it tells us that the problem is within individual schools, at a local level, where citizens can observe its operation and can take part in changing it. But large-scale studies like the Coleman and Jencks analyses cannot discover the social processes within schools that create inequality. If we are to address the sources of inequality in schools, then we must understand the phenomena that underlie Jencks's findings, and we must describe how they actually operate within schools.

This book attempts to overcome the limitations of previous large-scale studies by focusing on educational inequality in a systematic case study. This is the first study to describe the opportunity structure in a socially homogeneous school; consequently, this study is able to discover the pure effects of selection on socialization—quite apart from the effects of social class and racial biases. Being a detailed case study, this research is also able to discover the mechanisms underlying school selection: the subtle procedures that a school systematically uses to structure and define all students' opportunities. Furthermore, this study discovers a new model for the selection process—the tournament mobility model—wherein selection operates in successive stages, and this study shows that this model has important implications for students' awareness of selection and for the way they are socialized.

This study also investigates some of the assumptions underlying the "meritocracy" controversy, and it confronts the questions of whether or not meritocratic criteria exist and whether or not they are likely to be implemented. This study finds that, despite its meritocratic pretensions, the school actually uses different criteria than it claims to use—criteria which are inappropriate for these selections, but which are natural as choices for the school's gatekeepers to implement. It also finds that colleges inadvertently accept the school's inappropriate selections without realizing what criteria have gone into these selections. Finally, this study examines how the school deals with students' difficulties in accepting low-status positions. It discovers that the school evolves procedures and mythologies that influence students' development and that tend to create, exaggerate, and perpetuate social inequalities in school and society.

A theoretical chapter and a policy chapter conclude the book. The former provides a new perspective for understanding the way selection practices and unequal opportunity influence the socialization of youth. The discussion of tournament socialization offers a larger context for understanding the psychological concept of "expectancy effects", and it offers a new explanation for some recent findings about income and job status in sociology and economics. The final chapter provides a new analysis of the social policy issues involved in educational selection, and it proposes a systematic procedure for using "grass-roots research" to implement fundamental reforms.

I have tried to address this book to two kinds of readers. I have attempted to preserve the rigor of an academic monograph so that this study would contribute to the intellectual and theoretical issues concerning equality and selection currently being considered by economists, political scientists, psychologists, and sociologists. But these matters are also important to all citizens, and so I have addressed this book to them as well. I have attempted to relegate any social science terminology and complex statistics to footnotes as much as possible. The statistics and tables in the text are simple and straightforward, students in my undergraduate classes having helped make the text simpler and easier to understand.

This book addresses not only intellectual problems but also important social and political issues that concern all citizens. In recent years, parents, educators, and courts of law have become interested in educational selection. I hope this study will help all people who are concerned about social inequality and educational selection to understand how schools select and socialize youth for inequality and to find ways of reforming the selection practices in schools.

JAMES E. ROSENBAUM

Department of Sociology and Institution for Social and Policy Studies
Yale University
New Haven, Connecticut
February 1976

Acknowledgments

In writing this book, I have come to understand why an author refers to himself as "we." I learned that, for me, writing cannot be a solitary endeavor, for it is hard to continue writing without the intellectual and personal support of others. These others entered into my thoughts, both through real interactions and through imagined conversations. As I reread parts of this manuscript, I often asked myself, "What would they say about this idea?", and I found myself carrying on a fantasy dialogue with one of the many people who have contributed ideas to this work. Many people have read these chapters and given me valuable comments, and whatever value this book has is a tribute to them.

Lee Rainwater and Paul V. Smith, my mentors and friends, particularly influenced this work, by their insightful comments on my thoughts and drafts, by their continued commitment and attention, and, often most important, by the personal support they offered me throughout the past several years. The growth of this work, like my personal growth, has been profoundly influenced by these men, and I am deeply indebted to them.

I have received help from many others. Herbert Kelman, Gerald Lesser, Thomas Pettigrew, David Riesman, and Zick Rubin provided ideas and useful comments about the early stages of this work. As I first started setting my ideas out in early drafts, Chris Argyris, Geoffrey Bock, David Cohen, George Goethals, Christopher Jencks, Robert Rosenthal, and Virginia Warcholik helped me to find new ways to interpret my findings.

More recently, good fortune has brought me new colleagues who have contributed a great deal to the development of my thinking. Robert Althauser, Wendell Bell, Sarane Boocock, Lyn-Marie Craider, Janet Grigsby, Erik Hanushek, Nina Horowitz, William Kessen, Melvin Kohn, Murray Levine, Seymour Sarason, John Simon, Lisa Spungen, Harold Wechsler, and Stanton Wheeler have stimulated me to clarify my ideas. I am particularly grateful to John Low-Beer and David Stern, who have spent many hours discussing these issues with me and have suggested many useful ideas.

For the production of this work I am also indebted to many individuals. The key punching of the school record and questionnaire data was done by Dan Hellerstein and Mike O'Hare. Tapes of the student interviews were transcribed by Cathy Crockford, Linda Martinez, Anne Mihelich, Cathy Minicucci, and Virginia Warcholik. Rosemary Morazzini deserves particular recognition for her dedicated and able editing and typing of the many drafts of this manuscript. Having done some of the transcription, key punching, and typing myself, I know that such work can be interesting for brief periods, but that, over long stretches of time, it is only personal integrity that ensures accuracy, and I am most grateful to these people for the dedication they showed in making their contributions to this project.

I began this project as a study of students' attitudes to school, but as I became immersed in the school, I increasingly became aware of the more basic questions about the social reality of the school to which the students must respond. This awareness grew out of my interviews with the students, to whom I am grateful for giving so freely of their time and sharing their perceptions of the school. I am particularly indebted to four of these students (whom, regrettably, I cannot name, for the sake of the school's anonymity), with whom I spent a great deal of time, and whose awareness and insight into the dynamics of this school had a major impact on this study. The topic of this study and many of its discoveries originated from my conversations with them.

I was fortunate in being supported financially through much of this project. I was a fellow at the Joint Center for Urban Studies at Harvard and MIT for the first year of this work (1970), and the Joint Center provided me with personal and research support as well as a good atmosphere for learning more about urban affairs. I was an NIMH fellow during the second year of this work (1971) under grant number 1FO1 MH32899-01A2. NSF also provided me with research funds that enabled me to transcribe most of the interview tapes (Grant GS035337). The Social Relations Department and the Center for Law and Education provided me with computer funds for the data analysis reported here. During the last two years a grant from the Mary Babcock Foundation and the Institution for Social and Policy Studies at Yale University helped me to complete these analyses.

J. E. R.

Contents

Chapter 1   Tracks of Opportunity

The dialectic between opportunity and selection is a fundamental conflict in American society, but it is not a very open conflict. Most people know that selection processes operate in different stages of their lives, but they don't know how selections restrict their opportunities in far-reaching ways. Most people believe that schools are vital for providing opportunity and for creating meritocratic selections, but schools do not reveal how they accomplish these goals, if indeed they do. This reticence has led an increasing number of Americans to be suspicious of and disturbed about schools' selection procedures.

Parents worry that schools restrict their children's educational and social opportunities. In the past few years, more than two-thirds of state legislatures have noted this anxiety and have passed school accountability laws, many explicitly designed to prevent schools from closing off students' opportunities (Clasby et al., 1973). Courts of law have begun to consider questions of equal protection and due process in educational selection, particularly as these questions influence school selection criteria and students' rights to an effective say in choosing their own careers (Kirp, 1974). Moreover, an increasing number of social critics have begun to argue that schools exist, not to promote opportunity, accept the prospect of low social status. Relying on historical, sociological, and economic analyses, these critics contend that educational selection systems are less concerned with meeting educational goals than with socializing students' attitudes, personality traits, and behaviors in order to channel them into unrewarding work roles (Illich, 1970; Katz, 1971; Rothstein, 1971; Bowles and Gintis, 1973).

Although these worries have been disturbing, they have not yet been clearly articulated or well understood. Parents and legislators have addressed these issues only in regard to measures of school output (test scores and dropout statistics), without understanding how students' opportunities are defined inside schools. Courts have only recently begun to enter this domain, and a review of these cases concludes that the courts have not yet reached a clear formulation of school selection issues (Kirp, 1974). The radical social critics have raised provocative questions about opportunity and selection, but they have not presented sufficient research to specify or document many of their contentions.

This study investigates how these issues are dealt with inside a school. Most people are aware of the racial and social class discrimination in school selection. Yet this study goes beyond that, showing the difficulties that may be intrinsic to selection itself. This research examines a school where equal opportunity or meritocratic selection are possible, where the powerful biasing factors of racial and social class differences have been eliminated, and it asks how such a school resolves the conflicts between opportunity and selection.

This study follows students' careers as they proceed through school and into society and discovers the subtle methods a school uses to restrict students' opportunities without seeming to do so. It probes the school's selection criteria and observes that the school uses different criteria than it claims to use—criteria inappropriate for these selections but natural as choices for the school's gatekeepers to implement. It finds that colleges inadvertently accept a school's inappropriate selections without realizing what criteria have gone into them. This study also investigates how the school deals with students' difficulties in accepting low-status positions. It discovers that the school evolves procedures and mythologies that affect students' development and tend to create, exaggerate, and perpetuate social inequalities in school and society. Finally, this study not only strives to probe and understand these issues but also to propose some practical steps for reform. This research has been designed so that it might even become an instrument for remedying the problems of school selection.

Coleman, Jencks, and the Need for Structural Analysis of School Selection.   The Coleman Report (1966) and Jencks's book *Inequality* (1972), two of the most extensive studies of educational selection ever conducted, conclude that many of the important effects of educational selection occur inside schools. Coleman and Jencks probed the influence of schools on opportunity and inequality in society, and their results indicate that none of the many factors which they investigated (including resources, racial and social class composition, etc.) has a significant effect on students' cognitive outcomes, educational attainment, occupational status, or income.[1] When Jencks states that "differences between schools are . . . relatively small compared to . . . differences within the same school" (*Ibid.*, p. 106), many people infer that he is saying that nothing makes any difference. But that is not what Jencks concludes. Although he holds that most factors representing differences between schools do not have any effects, he also demonstrates that the selection system *within* schools (commonly called *tracking*) "is the one measurable factor that influences [educational] attainment" *(Ibid.,* p. 159). Coleman's and Jencks's studies point to selection within schools as an important determinant of school outcomes.

Unfortunately, Coleman's and Jencks's investigations could not go any further with this discovery. They analyze large surveys which are appropriate for studying gross differences between schools but which are not as appropriate for studying differences within schools. Furthermore, there are serious questions about the validity of the data they do obtain on selection within schools. For example, school administrators' responses about their selection systems often directly contradict most teachers' and students' responses in the same schools (Coleman, 1966, p. 569; Jencks, 1972, p. 97).[2] Evidently, administrators do not respond honestly to questions about educational selection in large-scale surveys; researchers must study this selection firsthand to be certain of the validity of their data.

The analyses of Coleman and Jencks have taken us down the path of large-scale surveys, and that path has led to the need for case studies. Having focused on schoolwide differences across the nation, their analyses suggest the need for a fresh start, for a study concentrating on the selection structure in a single school.

A case study of school selection has several advantages. First, it can help us interpret the mechanisms underlying the Coleman-–Jencks analyses. Coleman and Jencks estimate the average effects of variables, but they do not describe social mechanisms or tell us how these variables exercise their influence. Systems often create structures in order to control people without exerting force. For example, if society wants to keep cars on the road, it either could have police patrol all sidewalks or it could construct high curbs. The latter is both more effective and less expensive. Similarly, social structures are built to channel people to social positions without explicitly telling some to be doctors and others to be trash collectors. As we shall see, a school's track system can control students' opportunities without having to rely on blatant coercion. A case study can describe these processes.

Second, a case study of school selection permits the interpretation of empirical results departing from expectations. Curved trajectories for billiard balls are understandable only when we realize that the billiard table's surface is warped. Similarly, when Jencks's analyses do not explain students' careers after school, then the description of school selection procedures may help us interpret these results.

A third reason for studying school selection at close range is that it is the first stage of a general process that will occur over and over again throughout society. Societal institutions are continually selecting people for success and failure, and these selections define the opportunities that society offers its citizens and the way people are socialized in society. Yet societal selections occur in less visible and less simple settings than school selections. School selection is a simple prototype of this process, and it takes place within a single institution in plain view of the researcher, as if it were on the stage of his microscope. We can learn a great deal about the structure, process, and consequences of societal selections by looking at the selection structure within the school.

A case study of school selection not only responds to practical policy concerns, but it also addresses important theoretical questions about the nature of society. It may elucidate the social mechanisms which affect students' opportunities and socialization, it may explain empirical observations which deviate from theoretical predictions, and it may provide a model for the way stratification selects, channels, and socializes individuals in society.

What Is Tracking? Educational textbooks define two kinds of selection practices that are applied to most students in American schools. Ability grouping selects students on the basis of ability, differentiates instruction by quantity and intensity of work, and attempts "to suit the work to each student's unique intellectual

abilities" (Thomas and Thomas, 1965, p. 97). Curriculum grouping selects students on the basis of their educational and occupational plans and differentiates instruction according to the

> interests, desires, and ambitions [of students, and attempts to
> offer] . . . opportunities for those who wish to step from high
> school right into a job, on the one hand, and to also offer oppor-
> tunities for those who propose to start . . . college (Conant, 1967, p.
> 40).

Thus ability grouping is supposed to select students for instruction but not allocate them to college or jobs; while curriculum
grouping is supposed to allocate students to college and jobs but
not be selective (not exclude any students whose "interests, desires, and ambitions" bring them to seek a given curriculum).

Although ability grouping and curriculum grouping are
defined as different educational practices, they share two important social characteristics:

1. Students are grouped with those who are similar to themselves
   and separated from those who are different.
2. Grouping is based, at least in part, on a ranked criterion-
   —ability or postschool plans (college is considered superior to
   jobs); thus groups are unequal in status.

Although ability groups and curriculum groups may differ when
viewed from a pedagogical perspective, sociologists would consider them both to be hierarchical social structures.

I shall define tracking as any school selection system that attempts to homogenize classroom placements in terms of students'
personal qualities, performances, or aspirations. Thus tracking is
a general term that includes both ability grouping and curriculum grouping and emphasizes their social similarities.

Educators seem to have overlooked these similarities, and,
indeed, they are often unclear about what tracking is. In addition
to contradicting students and teachers on the Coleman questionnaire, principals also contradict themselves. Nearly all principals

answering the questionnaire claim that their schools provide curriculum groups (question P. 78), and yet in a following question many of them deny that their schools "carry out grouping or tracking of students according to ability or achievement" (question P. 80). This contradiction in successive questions probably does not represent an attempt at deception, but it does present a confusing picture, for curriculum placement is generally based on achievement (see U.S. Office of Education, 1962). This may manifest principals' confusion about tracking, a confusion apparently widespread among educators and social scientists. Most textbooks on educational administration describe curriculum grouping as a good administrative procedure and tracking as a bad (or controversial) one, but the two are never compared, and they usually do not even appear in the same chapter.[3]

This confused separation is not merely a small matter of pedagogical interest. By never comparing ability grouping and curriculum grouping, educators can avoid considering the possibility that their pedagogical procedures create a selection system which limits opportunity. Obviously, lack of attention to this possibility does not make it go away, and this is precisely the reason why careful examination of tracking is required.

Educational Research on Tracking. Educational research on tracking contains some of the best field data in social science. School grades and standardized test results are recorded over students' school careers, providing several indices of intellectual development over time. The school's centralized decision-making structure provides the essential prerequisite for an ideal experimental research design—a high degree of centralized control over matched groups—and it does so in a real-world setting.

But this research has several limitations, most stemming from its narrow focus and its lack of theoretical perspective. The question most often asked in such research from the 1920's to the 1970's was whether homogeneous grouping produces greater gains in achievement than heterogeneous grouping does. Even if researchers came to a clear answer to that question, they still would not know why the inferior system produces inferior achievement, nor would they know how to improve either system.

The second limitation of this research lies in its empirical results. As the several reviews of this massive literature conclude, these studies produce highly contradictory results (Otto, 1950; Goodlad, 1960; Borg, 1966; NEA, 1968; Heathers, 1969; Findley and Bryan, 1971). For example, NEA's (1968, p. 42) careful tabulation of the results of the 50 best controlled studies published since 1960 shows that, for each study exhibiting a net gain in achievement, a comparable study recorded a net loss (for all ability levels except the lowest, which had slightly more losses than gains). Several reviewers tried to retrieve some tendency from the research, but even these conclusions are contradictory. Several early reviewers conclude that

> the greatest relative effectiveness of ability grouping appeared to be for "dull" children, the next greatest for average children and the least (frequently harmful) for bright children (Findlay and Bryan, 1970, p. 24, summarizing Otto, 1950).

Yet, by the end of the 1960's, Borg (1966), Heathers (1969), and Findley and Bryan (1971) had concluded quite the opposite:

> ability grouping [is found] to be associated with gains for rapid learners that were offset by losses for slower learners. This is a case of the rich getting richer and the poor getting poorer (Heathers, 1969, p. 566).

The financial metaphor is appropriate for describing these educational studies. But accounting is certainly an inadequate method of assessment when the various auditors cannot even decide where the losses and gains are!

Unfortunately, because of its narrow focus, this research does not allow us to interpret the conflicting results. It tells us that tracking leads to very different achievement outcomes, but because it ignores tracking structures and social context, we cannot analyze why gains occur at some times and losses at other times. It

good for introduction

also ignores the process by which tracking operates, and so we do not even know whether the stated track policy is effectively implemented. If this research had been conceived more theoretically, if its aim had been to understand how tracking actually operates, then we would be in a much better position to understand why contradictions occur and what they signify.

Sociological Research on Tracking.   In contrast to the educational research on tracking, sociological research has taken a broader and more theoretical perspective, and it has produced more interesting results. Hollingshead's *Elmtown's Youth* (1949) provides an excellent study of the structure and process of tracking. Using a case study of a single school, Hollingshead is able to study the school structure in depth and to gain a comprehensive understanding of its operation. He describes the permanence of track placement, its selection criteria, and some of its social consequences. Hollingshead showed sociologists how social class differences pervade many aspects of school selection, creating discrimination and inextricably confounding tracking with social class. This lesson was so indelibly implanted in sociology that few sociological studies of schooling in the last quarter century have ignored social class effects.

Schafer and Olexa (1971) extend Hollingshead's work by illustrating how tracking embodies social class differences and affects student behaviors. Having access to the official school records, the researchers are able to investigate these cases in detail. They report that tracking is biased against lower-class students and that, even after controlling for social class, these lower-track placements lead students to misconduct, delinquency, grade decreases, and dropping out of school. They suggest that tracking is important in socializing lower-track students to delinquent roles and in excluding them from opportunities in society. Yet, unfortunately, because they obscure most of their analyses by combining the results from schools that differ markedly (e.g., in size, social class, racial composition, and track proportions), we cannot know whether tracking or the marked differences among schools account for the pooled results.[4] Furthermore, although they have access to longitudinal school records, they analyze data at only a single point in time (except grades). This not only leads to the usual difficulty of inferring causality but also means that their analyses present only a static portrayal of tracking.

Heyns (1974) provides a milestone in tracking research, demonstrating that the apparent social class biases in tracking are not what they seem. She studies the relative influences of social class background and achievement test scores on track placements. Using regression analyses on a sample of schools in the Coleman survey, she notes that social class is related to track placement only because of the class biases of achievement test scores; social class has no bearing per se. She suggests that tracking is rather meritocratic in most schools and that the apparent social class biases of tracking only reflect social class differences in achievement test performance. She implies that the tracking literature's preoccupation with social class biases may have been misdirected. Although tracking may not be *directly* related to differences in social class background, it may create a system of privilege within the school. Indeed, Heyns demonstrates that even after controlling for social class biases, tracking offers upper-track students better guidance counseling. Although her survey data do not allow her to examine this issue further, they suggest that tracking might have important influences, even if it does not reflect social class differences.[5]

What remains to be investigated is how tracking operates when not influenced by social class differences. The studies by Hollingshead, Schafer and Olexa, and others describe the opportunity structure, selection criteria, and social consequences of track systems, but they cannot separate the influence of social class from that of tracking itself. Coleman, Jencks, and Heyns separate them abstractly by means of statistical controls, but this does not permit us to see what is happening and why. What is needed is a detailed study of the structure and process of tracking in a socially homogeneous community, so that we can see how tracking operates when it is not distorted by social class differences.

The Issues of This Study.   This study does describe the structure
and process of tracking in a socially homogeneous community. By
taking a sociological perspective and considering in what ways
tracking might be a hierarchical social structure, this study raises
questions about tracking which are of fundamental theoretical
and practical importance.

1.   *How does track selection influence students' opportunities?*

Previous literature has not addressed this basic issue with any
clarity, and clarity is precisely what is required. Educational textbooks have offered confusing definitions, and educational research has studied only narrow outcomes. This lack of clarity
conceals and obscures the important effects schools may have on
students' career opportunities. Sociological research has pointed
out how social class and racial differences affect tracking, but it
has not described tracking itself (apart from discrimination), nor
has it studied the way tracking operates over time.

This study has carefully selected a setting where the effects of
social class and racial discrimination have been eliminated and
where tracking is likely to have particularly great importance
(Chapter 2). Therefore, this study is in an especially good position
to describe and analyze the opportunity structure of tracking.
Does tracking serve only pedagogical aims or does it also restrict
students' opportunities within the school? What mobility patterns
does a track system permit? How do the various tracks relate to
the colleges and jobs students enter after graduation? I shall
analyze the opportunity structure within the school (Chapter 3)
and its effects on opportunity in society (Chapter 5).

2.   *Upon what criteria does a school base track selections?*

Recent popular arguments have heralded the coming of a
"meritocracy" as a justification for restricted opportunity (see
Herrnstein, 1971). It is somewhat comforting to think that the
most talented people get the top positions in society (perhaps

particularly comforting to college professors), and yet
Herrnstein's argument is weak, being based only on simple correspondences between IQ and jobs. Because many other factors
correlate with IQ and jobs (e.g., social background, education,
etc.), we cannot interpret Herrnstein's correspondences as indicating a causal relationship without controlling for these other
factors and finding the intervening mechanisms.

Schools are generally assumed to be the primary mechanism
for implementing meritocracy. The meritocracy argument is
often premised on the assumption that schools actually use
meritocratic criteria, both for selecting students for advanced
preparation and for allocating them to societal positions. Indeed,
since job requirements often explicitly state the importance of
school preparation and credentials, we may infer that societal
meritocracy is somewhat dependent on school selection being
meritocratic.

As we have noted, Heyns suggests that track placements tend
to be relatively meritocratic, but, because she did not have access
to the schools' own records of ability and achievement, she was
unable to determine precisely how schools implement their
criteria. Cicourel and Kitsuse's (1963) research is virtually the
only study of this topic. They find that schools are rather
haphazard about the way they implement school criteria, unsys-
tematically choosing among various official criteria and subjective
impressions in making these placements. If these data are
generalizable, then they suggest that schools are not meritocratic.
Yet the small size of the lower track in their school (only 9 of the
78 students in their sample were in the noncollege track) reduces
the possibilities for detailed analysis, diminishes the impact of
their findings, and even suggests that lower-track placements are
anomalous and based on unusual criteria (an inference supported by their interviews with guidance counselors).

My study replicates and goes beyond their study, directly con-
fronting tracking's meritocratic assumptions. Chapter 4 investigates some fundamental issues overlooked in the meritocracy
debate. What selection criteria does a school use for determining

students' opportunities in school? Are they used in the same way over time? Are they appropriate for making these selections? Chapter 5 investigates to what extent selection criteria influence the way students are channeled into society. Chapter 6 investigates the role of choice in selection. Analysis of these issues reaches some surprising conclusions and forces a reappraisal of the possibilities for meritocracy.

3.   *How does track selection socialize students?*

Sociologists have speculated that social structures influence socialization, but the social structures of societies are generally too complex for clearly defining this influence. A track system provides a microcosm for studying the influence of a social structure on socialization. By studying a clearly defined track system in a socially homogeneous community, we can discern how the social structure of tracking creates distinct social environments, defines interpersonal expectations and interactions, and influences the roles and capacities students acquire. Our approach leads us to expect tracking to have more profound and different effects than the simple achievement gains previous research has noted, and we find that tracking actually influences students' IQs in ways that support the operation of the track system (Chapter 7). Furthermore, the social structure model of tracking leads to an investigation of tracking's effects on students' school participation, friendship choices, and social stereotypes, and to the discovery of the role of the selection mythology in creating, exaggerating, and perpetuating social inequalities in school and society (Chapter 8). These analyses suggest theoretical speculations about the ways society influences selection and the ways selection fosters socialization outcomes (Chapter 9).

These analyses also suggest speculations about another important issue. After seeing how the school defines different opportunity tracks and selects students to be placed in each, we must wonder how the school manages to get students to accept and fit into their placements. In particular, how does a school convince

some students to accept the prospect of having a low-status position in society? Obviously, a society that promises everyone opportunity but not success makes unfulfilled aspirations an inevitable outcome. Because the school track system is important in
defining and limiting students' opportunities, schools will also
have to deal with students' reactions to selection. The way schools
handle this issue is crucial for the legitimacy of society's inequalities. Chapter 9 considers how schools persuade lower-track
students to accept the prospect of restricted opportunity.

The final chapter (Chapter 10) explores the pertinence of
these findings for reforming school selection policies, proposes a
procedure for reform, and speculates on the implications of this
reform for socialization and social inequality.

Is This Case Generalizable?   The question of generalizability must
inevitably arise in any case study. It must be conceded at the
outset that the track system studied (hereafter referred to by the
pseudonym *Grayton*) cannot possibly represent all track systems.
American education is sufficiently decentralized and American
thinking on tracking is sufficiently diverse that there are probably
several major types of track system in this country. As we shall see
later, however, other studies suggest that important characteristics of this track system are not unique. Furthermore, although
the inadequacies of survey data imply that the question "How
typical?" cannot be precisely answered, detailed case studies such
as this are generalizable and can make important contributions to
a theory of tracking.

Some of the most striking characteristics of the Grayton track
structure—those that may prompt one to question its
typicality—have been noted by case studies of other schools.
Track systems in which student placements extend across several
subjects, allow downward but not upward changes, and preclude
substantial influence by student or parent choices have been
described in several studies of high schools (Hollingshead, 1949;
Sexton, 1961; Cicourel and Kitsuse, 1963; *Hobson* v. *Hansen*,
1967; Schafer and Olexa, 1971). Descriptions of tracking in each

are not specific or systematically documented, but they do suggest that the striking characteristics of the Grayton track structure are not totally atypical.

One-quarter of the principals in the Coleman Report sample said that their schools place students in the same track for all subjects. This attribute of the Grayton track system is rather widespread. Of course, we must be cautious in relying on these principals' responses, for it has already been noted that they are deceptive and confused. Ironically, although we are unable to know how typical the Grayton track system is from the Coleman Report data, these data clearly indicate that the administrative confusion and deception noted in Grayton are quite typical (see Chapter 3).

If we do not know what is typical among actual track systems, then typicality does not provide guidelines for selection of a track system. But there are other criteria to consider. A track system should be selected to maximize the possibility of discovering new findings, to maximize the generalizability of the findings, and to maximize understanding of the general process of tracking.

Sørensen (1970) has provided a set of sociological dimensions for defining track systems. As we shall see in Chapter 3, Grayton's track system fits into Sørensen's dimensions as low in inclusiveness (number of options) and electiveness (degree of choice) and higher in selectiveness (amount of homogeneity intended) and scope (extensiveness and permanence of placements). The Grayton track system represents an unambiguous position on each of these dimensions, and, in each case that position tends to maximize the school's regimentation of students' placements and minimize the school's responsiveness to an individual student's particular talents, needs, and choices. In this matrix of dimensions, the Grayton track system seems to represent the upper limit for the influence of tracking on student careers and development. Furthermore, because Grayton is a homogeneous, white, working-class community, this study manifests the effects of tracking independent of social class and racial differences.

Because Sørensen's dimensions have never been applied to an

actual track system, this case study is useful for clarifying them, for example, by illustrating the way they are manifested concretely and the difficulty of putting them into operation. Applying Sørensen's dimensions to a track system that is so extreme on them is particularly useful, for it makes them even more salient, demonstrates their interrelations, and even suggests new dimensions that Sørensen did not consider (e.g., direction of track change). Selection of the Grayton track system maximizes, therefore, the contribution of this case study to a general theory of tracking. Furthermore, the confusion of the principals' responses (and the researchers' questions) in the Coleman survey can be eliminated only after case studies like this one have clarified what tracking is.

The extreme position of the Grayton track system in the matrix of possibilities also offers some unique opportunities for discovery and generalization, as can be seen in two examples.

1. Studying the Grayton track system permits the discovery of new, unexpected outcomes. Although researchers have studied the effects of tracking on mean IQ with very mixed results over several decades, this is the first study to detect the differentiation and homogenization of IQ. This discovery leads to provocative inferences about the socialization processes in tracking (Chapter 7).

2. Because of the extensiveness and permanence of track placements in Grayton, their effect on jobs is likely to be stronger in Grayton than in other track systems. Since this study finds that track placement has very little effect on jobs, other track systems, which do not create such early determined and specialized vocational tracks, are even less likely to have an effect on jobs (Chapter 5).

Therefore the particular properties of the Grayton track system increase the generalizability of some findings and facilitate the discovery of other findings (which require caution in generalization).

The Practical Uses of a Case Study: Grass-Roots Research.   The recent trend in social policy research has been toward large-scale surveys, yet few unequivocal conclusions, and even fewer practical policies, have resulted from such research. Even when agreeing on methodological issues and using the same data, researchers can arrive at contradictory interpretations [compare Bowles (1972) with Jencks et al.]. Furthermore, even if clear results were produced, reformers would have difficulty in implementing them in their communities. Because the findings would be probabilistic, one could not be certain that they applied to a particular community; because they would be static, one might not understand what actions to take to change the situation; because they would be abstract, one would have difficulty in using them to motivate community concern. Consequently, large-scale surveys are unlikely to produce effective policy reform.

"More research" is the cliché researchers append to their conclusions to admit the modesty of their contribution (and, possibly, their doubts about its validity). I shall propose more research at the outset of this work, but a different kind of research. I propose "grass-roots research"—that people concerned about educational selection conduct research themselves to understand the way selection operates in their own schools. Such studies would scientifically replicate these findings or discern in what circumstances these findings hold. But they would also serve practical purposes: specifying the precise selection issues in a particular school, suggesting policy implications, and mobilizing community involvement. This study provides methods that community people can use to investigate and reform selection in their own schools.[6]

But probably the primary value of this study is as a model for conceptualizing selection issues and for suggesting the dilemmas endemic to selection. Particularly because of its specific characteristics, this case study can indicate many of the *potential* pitfalls of *any* system involving classification, selection, or allocation. It considers many aspects of selection: mobility patterns, appropriateness and consistency of selection criteria, opportunities after graduation, the coopting role of misled choice, and the influence of selection structures on socialization and social behavior. All provide potential risks. Although the findings of this case study are not always generalizable, they are always potential risks, and this study can help readers know what to look for and how to understand selection in their own experience. Educators, parents, lawyers, and social scientists need to understand the properties and consequences of selection, and this case study presents these issues in a clear and concrete form.

NOTES

1. The Coleman Report dealt only with cognitive outcomes and educational attainment. Jencks et al. addressed both educational and occupational outcomes. For reviews and reanalyses of the Coleman Report the reader is referred to the *Harvard Educational Review*, special issue on "Equal Educational Opportunity" (Vol. 38, No. 1, Winter, 1968) and Mosteller and Moynihan (1972). For reviews of Jencks, the reader is referred to the *Harvard Educational Review*, special issue on "Perspectives on Inequality" (Vol. 43, No. 1, February, 1973).

2. Jencks also concedes that measures of track placements may not be valid, and it is regrettable that the Coleman data do not offer trustworthy independent measures of this variable (Jencks et al., 1972, p. 174, No. 71).

3. The term *tracking* has been used by educators for some time, but their usage has tended to be rather vague and contradictory. At times *tracking* has been used to refer to ability groups (Thomas and Thomas, 1965, p. 130; Conant, 1967, p. 30) and at other times to curriculum groups (Tanner, 1965, p. 221).

    Despite differences in definition, these two selection practices are likely to be highly similar. Although ability tracking is not defined to have any influence on college or jobs, educators generally feel that college and job allocations should be meritocratic; we might, therefore, expect high-ability-group students to get preference when educators make such allocations. Similarly, we might expect educators' meritocratic beliefs to lead to curriculum tracks' being selective and related to ability. Indeed, a national survey (U.S. Office of Education, 1962) indicates that curriculum tracking is highly related to IQ. Contrary to definition, curriculum tracking, in fact, performs a selection function. The selection and allocation functions of schools may be related, and both may be promoted in any school's grouping system.

Although educators have used the term in conflicting ways, noneducators have begun to avoid the distinctions and include both kinds of grouping in the meaning of tracking. Thus sociologists (Sexton, 1961; Schafer and Olexa, 1971; Heyns, 1971); jurists (Hall, 1970; Kirp, 1973); and radical critics of schools (Rothstein, 1971) have all used the term in this general way.

4. The authors' method of controlling for background factors is also misleading. To ascertain the relationship between two factors while controlling for a third, the authors "sorted, or controlled, on each variable; then percentages were computed for each resulting category"; then weighted percentages were computed (*ibid.*, p. 35). A multiple regression analysis would have been far more appropriate.

5. Heyns was one of Jencks's colleagues in the preparation of *Inequality,* and her analyses of tracking form the basis of most of the discussion of track placement in that book. Although her methods are sophisticated and well implemented, the previously cited inadequacies of *Inequality* also apply to Heyns's work. Because Coleman's data lack reliable information on differences within schools and lack longitudinal data, Heyns's effort to understand processes within schools must rely on students' statements. Of course, both Heyns and Jencks are aware of the possibility that some students may perceive things incorrectly or distort their reports to praise or

criticize the school. Jencks et al. (1972, p. 174, No. 71) concede that students' perceptions of their track placements may not be valid and students' statements about the guidance they receive may be doubted, and Heyns (1971, Chapter 2) also discusses some of the validity problems.

6. This study is quite easily replicated. For the most part it relies on data gathered directly from the school's own records, and most schools collect comparable data. Furthermore, it mostly uses simple statistical analyses, which are easily reproduced by someone with elementary skills in data analysis.

Chapter 2   The Selection of a Setting

C hoosing the setting for a case study is of paramount importance. The aim of this chapter is to delineate the setting required for this study, to describe the setting and the sample chosen, and then, to demonstrate that the choices meet the requirements.

The Requirements For a Setting. Social research has repeatedly shown that a student's track placement is highly related to his social background. Hollingshead's classic study, *Elmtown's Youth* (1949), pointed out that high school track placement virtually reproduced the social class structure of the community. Subsequent studies have demonstrated over and over that social class and racial background are important influences on the selection of youth for track placements (Schafer and Olexa, 1971) and into positions in society (Kahl, 1953; Lipset and Bendix, 1959). Social class and racial background seem to affect selection in many ways—through test scores, teacher expectations, privileges, connections, and "pull"—and at many different times throughout a youth's school and job career.

The interaction of these factors is interesting but also complex. Because this study is concerned with the operation of tracking as such, it was decided at the outset to select a socially homogeneous setting in which social class and racial differences would not complicate and interact with the track system. In this decision, there was no intent to belittle the importance of social class and racial differences; on the contrary, the intent was to state from the outset that they are so influential at every stage of tracking that they prevent a clear understanding of tracking.

There remains the choice of which social class to study. Wilson (1959) and Sexton (1961) have pointed out that the social class composition of a school has some bearing on its operation and outcomes. In many upper-middle-class schools, college attendance seems to be assured (see Cicourel and Kitsuse, 1963), while in many lower-class high schools, few, if any, graduates attend college (Morland, 1964). Only in schools between these extremes—in middle- and working-class schools—is college attendance an uncertainty: possible but not assured. Tracking would be expected to exert the greatest influence on students' life chances in such schools.

The choice of a working-class school has two other advantages. First, several studies have demonstrated that college attendance is most closely related to merit criteria in working-class settings (Kahl, 1953). Since one aim of this study is to investigate whether track placements and college attendance can fit the meritocratic ideal, the choice of a working-class community increases the likelihood that this setting will resemble the meritocratic ideal. If so, this study will be able to describe the operation of a meritocratic selection process.

Another advantage to studying such a setting is that college attendance is particularly important for the life chances of working-class students who lack other means of attaining middle-class jobs (e.g., personal contacts). As Lipset and Bendix conclude from their study of intergenerational mobility, "only college education enables manual workers' sons to enter the labor market in a middle class occupation" (1959, p 197).

The Setting and the Sample.   A town, which I shall call Grayton, was selected from the Boston metropolitan area. Like many of the residential communities in Boston, Grayton's population is about 100,000 and predominantly white, working-class, first- or second-generation Irish and Italian. The census reports that fewer than 500 of Grayton's inhabitants are nonwhite and that, whereas 20% of the work force of Boston are in professional or managerial jobs, only 12% of Grayton's work force are in these categories. At the other end of the scale, more than 20% of Boston's work force are in service or labor positions, but only 14% of Grayton's work force are in these unskilled jobs.

Grayton high school, which absorbs most, but not all, of the school-age youth in the city, is a three-year high school (tenth through twelfth grades) with about 2300 students. Virtually all the population of Grayton is Catholic, and the parochial high schools in the Boston vicinity are said to provide a better education than the Grayton public high school does. Yet few residents of Grayton can afford the tuition at the parochial schools; therefore, few of Grayton's youth attend them. Like the schools in most working-class communities, Grayton's 40% dropout rate is high when compared with high schools across the country (see Jencks, 1972, p. 156). These factors would lead us to expect that the social class backgrounds of students in Grayton high school would be even more homogeneous than the entire population of the town. The parochial schools are likely to take students from relatively affluent families, and the dropout rate is likely to take its toll on students from lower-class backgrounds.

A questionnaire asking parents' education and occupations was administered to a random sample of twelfth grade history classes (see Appendix). The job distribution of the fathers of these students is only slightly more homogeneous than the census data for the town: 12% have professional or managerial jobs and 10% have unskilled jobs. The census indicates that 74% of the town hold semiskilled or skilled jobs or own and operate small businesses, and this sample reports 78% having fathers with such jobs. This suggests that the school sample is only slightly more homogeneous than the town as a whole.

The students' responses regarding parents' education revealed similar homogenity: 14% of the fathers completed less than nine years of school and only 9% finished college. The variation in mothers' education is even more restricted. There was no need to ask race: only 3 of the 192 respondents in the various classrooms were Blacks, and no other race was represented. This survey affirms that the social class and racial composition of the senior class in Grayton high school was much like that of the town: homogeneously white and working class.

Organizational Characteristics of the School.   Grayton high school, physically resembling many urban schools, is a two-story red brick building constructed around the turn of the century, with several wings subsequently added. The areas students occupy allow neither comfort nor privacy. Long, undecorated corridors are regularly broken by stark and dismal classrooms. Many of the windows are cracked, and the scratched and decrepit desks are bolted to the floor. There is no student lounge. The teachers fare little better. There is a small teachers' lounge filled with dilapidated furniture, lacking even the convenience of a coffee urn. In the entire building, only the principal's and guidance counselors' offices are roomy and comfortable.

The physical features of the building symbolize the organization of the school. Students have no power and few rights or privileges. Teachers are granted more prerogatives, but the real authority resides with the principal and the guidance counselors.

The records of all students flow through the offices of five administrators (the principal plus four guidance counselors appointed by him), and implementation of the track system is solely their responsibility. Teachers can make recommendations, but all decisions are made by these men. They collect school records, interview students, assign track placements, and have the power and authority to formulate and administer any track policy they choose. The track system described in the following chapters is the product of the policies formulated and implemented by these men.

Social Class Influence on Track Placement and College Attendance.   This chapter began by stipulating that a setting was required that would minimize the influence of social class and racial differences, and Grayton was selected with this in mind. Although Grayton is very homogeneous, it is not completely homogeneous in social class. To what extent do the observed differences in parents' education and occupations influence the operation of the Grayton track system?

The track system will be described in greater detail in the next chapter. For this analysis, it is necessary only to specify the most basic track distinction: between the college and noncollege tracks. The comparable distinction in societal positions is between college attendance and nonattendance. Nearly half (48%) of the ninth grade students in this sample are in the college track and nearly a third (32%) attend a four-year college after graduation.

Already one limitation on the possible effects of social class is apparent. Even if the track system were completely biased in favor of the upper-middle-class students, only 12% of the sample come from such families, and this cannot explain the half of the sample in college track or the third that attend college.

The actual situation shows even less influence by these factors than the limited amount possible. Students having college-educated parents are no more likely to be in college tracks than are those whose parents have less than 12 years of education; half of each group is in college tracks. Students whose fathers have professional or managerial jobs are somewhat more likely to be in college tracks than in noncollege tracks (64%). Students whose

fathers hold unskilled jobs are just as likely to be in college tracks as in noncollege tracks. Clearly, there is little bias by fathers' education or job status.

The situation is similar for college attendance. Indeed, multiple regressions indicate that father's education, father's occupation, mother's education and mother's occupation explain less than 2% of the variance of track placement or college attendance. Clearly, this track system is not significantly influenced by social class factors.

It is so unusual to discover a school that exhibits so little social class bias that these findings, although welcome, are perplexing. There are several possible reasons for these anomalous data. Students' reports of their parents' education and occupations could be distorted, but this is unlikely, for they reported the same information in face-to-face interviews several months later. Two other possibilities are more likely. It seems likely that a professional or managerial occupation in a working-class community signifies different social class characteristics than it does in an upper-middle-class community. Warner's scale of social class (1949) makes this distinction by including the quality of housing in the social class index. It also seems reasonable to expect that a homogeneous school like Grayton would be less responsive to its small social class differences than more heterogeneous schools would be toward their more extreme differences. Whatever the reason, these data clearly indicate that social class factors do not exert much of an influence on track placement or college attendance for Grayton students.

These data apply only to those students who attended the public high school and did not drop out before twelfth grade. There may be marked social class differences in the track placements of students in an earlier grade. This study will, however, limit its focus to the operation of tracking on students who stay within the public high school.

Conclusion. This discovery of a lack of social class bias in this school may be taken as the first finding of this study. We are so accustomed to seeing school placements' being affected by parents' education and jobs that we are sometimes uncautious and ignore the possibility of limiting cases. Grayton high school is just such a limiting case. It does not challenge previous wisdom but illustrates that there are limits to its generality.

This chapter's most important conclusion is that Grayton high school represents an ideal setting for the study of tracking. The population is completely homogeneous racially and largely homogeneous socially. Moreover, the social class differences that do exist do not seem to exert a significant influence on track placement or college attendance. Therefore, the study of tracking in Grayton will indicate the way tracking operates when it is not influenced by social class or racial differences. Furthermore, because this is a working-class community, track placement and college attendance are particularly important, for they have significant influences on the life chances of these students.

APPENDIX: THE DATA FOR THIS STUDY

This study is based on three kinds of data, permitting diverse perspectives on tracking. The main source of the data was the Grayton high school records, which provide indicators of track placement, ability test scores, grades, attendance, and teachers' ratings of industry, deportment, and ability (see Chapter 4 for a more nearly complete description). Since these data are available for all students in the class of 1971, any analysis using just these data could be done on the entire class ($n = 457$). Chapters 3 and 7 use the entire class of 1971 as the "sample."

Additional data were gathered in a questionnaire that asked about educational expectations (Chapter 6) and parents' educational and occupational attainment (Chapter 2). It was administered to a random sample of one-third of the history classrooms in each track, a sample selected to have an equal number of students from college and noncollege tracks at the onset of high school (actually 48%). Therefore, this sample overrepresents the college track, since only 35% of the entire class is actually in college track. This sample of 192 students is used for the analyses in Chapters 2, 3, 4, 5, 6, and 8.

A stratified random sample of 50 seniors (20 college, 10 business, and 20 general track) were interviewed. The interview sample was selected from the questionnaire sample. The interviews took about two hours and used open-ended questions. They dealt with students' aspirations and expectations, their experiences and careers through school, their friendships and after-school activities, and their perceptions of tracking. This sample is used for the analyses in Chapters 3, 6, 8, and 9.

Chapter 3   Opportunity and Tracking

Social mobility research has rarely considered the selection systems within schools and their influence on youth's opportunities in society. Many researchers have looked at schoolwide effects (Coleman et al., 1966; Jencks et al., 1972; Heyns, 1974) and have observed that differences within schools are much greater than those among schools, but their data did not permit them to investigate the selection systems within schools. Indeed, the Coleman Report's effort to obtain information on this topic revealed that administrators' statements on tracking often contradicted those of teachers and students (Coleman, 1966, p. 569; Jencks, 1972, p. 97). These contradictory reports illustrate the need for case studies within schools, for discovering both the actual selection system and the reason for the conflicting reports.

Ralph Turner (1960) provides a conceptual perspective for such an endeavor in an essay that continues to be influential in sociology and education. He has proposed two ideal types to describe normative patterns of social mobility within British and American societies—the sponsored and contest mobility norms. In the sponsored norm, which Turner attributes to Britain, students are selected for elite status at an early time; and they are maximally separated, provided with specialized training and socialization, and guaranteed that they—and only they—will have the opportunity for elite status in society. The contest norm, which Turner attributes to the United States, delays and minimizes selection, separation, specialized treatment, and restrictions on opportunity. Of course, even in a contest system, selections must sometimes occur, but this system delays them and minimizes their consequences. Thus, when American high schools begin tracking, Turner notes that they try "to avoid any sharp social separation between the superior and inferior students and to keep the channels of movement between courses of study as open as possible" (ibid., p. 860). The contest system instills an "insecurity of elite position. In a sense, there is no final arrival under contest mobility, since each person may be displaced by newcomers throughout his life" (ibid., p. 859). On the other hand, the contest norm strives to minimize the occurrence of losers "keeping everyone in the running" by offering remedial help to the less successful within the schools and by providing junior colleges that offer "many students 'a second chance' to qualify for university" (ibid., p. 861).

Turner's main aim is to describe the normative patterns affecting the relationship of education and opportunity, but beyond his preoccupation with norms he devotes considerable attention to administrative policies and institutional structures: the British "eleven plus" exam, the American comprehensive high school, remedial education, and junior colleges. Indeed, Turner concludes his essay with the provocative suggestion that "there is a constant 'strain' to bring the relevant features of the class system, the pattern of social control, and the educational system into consistency with the norm" (*ibid.*, p. 865). Considering his essay "more illustrative than demonstrative," he does not try to judge whether this "strain" actually results in consistency between the normative patterns and educational policies and practices.

Turner's essay is insightful, provocative, and persuasive. Sensitive to many nuances of American beliefs and practices, he relates these to data from attitude surveys to make a compelling, believable case for the applicability of the contest model.

The danger is that we may take it for more than it is. Turner intends the contest model to describe American norms—the way things are supposed to be. But we tend to assume that administrative policies are simply derived from norms and that policies are good descriptions of actual practices. Turner's allusions to policies and practices contribute to these assumptions (although that is not his intention). The prevalence of these assumptions may account for the absence of research on the actual opportunity structures within schools.

The task of this chapter is to test these assumptions. To what extent does the administrative policy of Grayton's track system resemble the contest norm?. To what extent does this policy describe the actual opportunity structure of the school? These are the primary issues of this chapter, and their answers will lead us to important new insights into educational opportunity.

The Norm and the Stated Policy. The Grayton administrators, guidance counselors, and official publications express considerable support for the contest mobility norm. The Grayton student handbook states:

> The school feels that diversity is basic to American democracy and this diversity can be useful in the students' learning and in their lives. Students should learn to understand one another. The gifted student should in some way know the problems of the slow learner.

Administrators and guidance counselors also express these sentiments, emphasizing the desirability of maintaining a "flexible curriculum." They feel that the curriculum should permit diverse students not only to mix with one another but also to feel they "have the opportunity to better themselves if they will settle down and try" (in the words of one administrator). One guidance counselor stated, "We do not decide students' opportunities after school: that isn't for us to decide. Students decide that themselves by their own performance throughout school." Clearly, the administrators and guidance counselors support the main tenets of the contest norm. Does this support lead to an administrative policy resembling that norm?

The simplest and most obvious description of the school's stated policy on opportunity is the sequence of opportunities presented to pupils and their parents throughout the pupil's school career. Pupils and their parents are allowed to make choices at various times and these choices define the options the school offers. The sequential pattern of students' options defines the opportunity structure of the school.

The administrators' description of the school's tracking policy makes it clear that the opportunity structure resembles the contest norm. The junior high administrators report that all students take virtually the same curriculum in the junior high school. The only differentiation is for a single elective slot that allows four options: foreign language, business training, industrial arts, and household arts.

The administrators report that tracking begins at the end of the ninth grade with the onset of senior high school. There are three different curricula (or tracks) in senior high: college, business, and general. Students choose one for the duration of their high school career, although the student handbook suggests that track changes are possible at any time. The handbook specifies some requirements for each track (such as language for college track or typing for business track), and yet very few courses are restricted to students in a single track. The handbook implies that there is considerable mixing of students from different tracks, but it does not specify how much mixing actually occurs.

I discussed these issues with the principal and guidance counselors. None could specify the degree of mixing of students from different tracks or the number of students who changed tracks, but each did assert that there was no policy to confine students to a single track, and each could cite examples of individuals who crossed tracks for different subjects or who changed tracks over time. Several administrators referred me to the student handbook passage already quoted that affirms the school's commitment to classroom diversity. From this statement, one would expect considerable effort to mix students. Furthermore, because all students have so many common requirements and electives, it would seem extremely likely that the boundaries between tracks would be highly permeable.

The stated policy seems to reflect the contest model by minimizing the divisions in the school, by maximizing options, and by maintaining free choice. The only division in the junior high is in a single course elective, and the divisions in the senior high permit diverse opportunities and considerable mixing across tracks. Free choice is emphasized in each division, and none of these decisions closes off the possibility of subsequent track change. Although the stated policy is vague, the image projected is that of a contest mobility system.

The Actual Track Structure in the Junior High School.   The actual records of the course assignments in the junior high school were not available for this study, but interviews with the staff and students in the senior high school provided some indication of this structure. These accounts might be considered dubious if it were not for the complete agreement among administrators, guidance counselors, teachers, and students (as opposed to the conflicting accounts the senior high respondents offered of their own school).

Despite the claims of the junior high administrators, there are actually nine tracks in each of the junior high years. The choice of a foreign language leads to placement in one of the first five tracks (labeled A to E); any other elective leads to placement in the last four tracks (F to I). Tracks are ranked within these two groups according to teachers' assessments and IQ scores.

Students in each track have all their classes together and even sit together at lunch and in assemblies. Furthermore, each class is paced by the ability level of the section. Thus the top language group has the most difficult history class, English class, and mathematics class. The second highest language group has a slightly easier class in each of these subjects, and so on. Moreover, language tracks have more difficult classes than nonlanguage tracks. There is a graduated scale of difficulty that applies to all the courses a student is taking.

This description is quite different from the image projected by the junior high school. The stated policy suggests that the foreign language elective is merely a choice of a single course. Yet in fact this choice determines both the group of students that a student is placed with for all his classes and the level of difficulty of all his classes. In addition, the division of ability level within these groups is decided by the school, and the stated policy does not even mention this.

The Actual Track System in the Senior High School.   The senior high school staff were considerably more evasive in describing the track system in their own school, and my interviews with them offered virtually no additional information beyond the stated policy described earlier. But I did manage to gain access to the school records for the entire class of 1971 ($n = 457$), which portray the same pattern as the junior high even more graphically.

Table 3.1, showing the enrollments for tenth grade English and history, demonstrates a very high correspondence between the track enrollments in these two subjects. Indeed, fewer than 5% of the students (22 of 451) are not in the same track in both subjects, and only 1% (5 students) are more than one track away.[1] Of course, English and history call for fairly similar skills, but correspondence between English and mathematics track placement does not point to much more flexibility (cf. Table 3.2). Overall, the number of students not in the same track in English

TABLE 3.1   TRACK PLACEMENTS FOR TENTH GRADE ENGLISH
AND HISTORY

English Track	History Track				
	Upper College (%)	Lower College (%)	Business (%)	Upper General (%)	Lower General (%)
Upper college	83.3	3.3	0.0	0.0	0.0
Lower college	16.7	96.0	0.5	0.0	1.5
Business	0.0	0.7	99.0	29.4	6.2
Upper general	0.0	0.0	0.0	70.6	3.1
Lower general	0.0	0.0	0.5	0.0	89.2
Total	100.0	100.0	100.0	100.0	100.0
Number of cases	(12)	(151)	(206)	(17)	(65)

χ^2 =   1326.9

Gamma   =   0.99

TABLE 3.2   TRACK PLACEMENTS FOR TENTH GRADE ENGLISH
AND MATHEMATICS

Math Track	English Track				
	Upper College (%)	Lower College (%)	Business (%)	Upper General (%)	Lower General (%)
Upper college	66.7	8.6	0.5	0.0	0.0
Lower college	33.3	83.6	0.5	29.4	4.4
General math	0.0	2.3	1.0	5.9	45.6
No math	0.0	5.5	98.0	64.7	50.0
Total	100.0	100.0	100.0	100.0	100.0
Number of cases	(12)	(128)	(204)	(17)	(68)

χ^2 =   577.1

Gamma   =   0.63

and mathematics is about twice that for English and history, but it
is still only 11% (46 of 429).

The main distinction in the track system is between the college
and noncollege tracks, and thus mixing between these tracks
might be considered a more meaningful indication of track separation. When English and history are compared, only 0.7% (3 of
452) cross tracks from college to noncollege tracks or vice versa.
When English and mathematics are compared 5% (20 of 429) are
in college tracks in one subject and noncollege tracks in the other.
Clearly, there is more mixing between English and mathematics
tracks than between English and history, but in neither is there
very much mixing. The actual track placements in the senior high
school may allow for individual exceptions, as the administrators
say, but these exceptions are just that. Most students are placed in
the same track in the three main academic subjects.

Patterns of Track Changes over Time.   The school records also
permit the analysis of patterns of track changes over time. Table
3.3, showing the track placements of students in the tenth and
eleventh grades (for English courses), demonstrates that there is
very little track change in this interval. The overwhelming majority of students stay in the same track in tenth and eleventh grades.

Furthermore, the changes that do occur fit a definite pattern.
Students rarely move up from noncollege to college tracks, but
they often move down. Although some move up, very few move
beyond the adjacent track, and fewer than 3% (8 of 292) change
from noncollege tracks into a college track. In contrast, 21% (35
of 163) of college track students change to a noncollege track in
the following year. Downward track change is thus more than
seven times as likely as upward.

This reflects student track changes over only one year. Table
3.4 shows track placements between ninth and twelfth grades for
a one-third random sample of these students.[2] In this three-year
interval, we see the same pattern of track change. Most students
do not change tracks. All those who do change move down in
tracks. None of the 53 noncollege track students move up into

TABLE 3.3   TRACK PLACEMENTS FOR TENTH AND ELEVENTH GRADE (ENGLISH CLASSES)

Eleventh Grade Track Placement	Tenth Grade Track Placement				
	Upper College (%)	Lower College (%)	Business (%)	Upper General (%)	Lower General (%)
Upper college	91.7	7.3	0.0	0.0	0.0
Lower college	8.3	69.5	2.4	11.8	1.5
Upper business	0.0	3.3	35.3	0.0	1.5
Lower business	0.0	14.6	60.4	29.4	10.3
Upper general	0.0	3.3	0.0	47.1	5.9
Lower general	0.0	2.0	1.9	11.8	80.9
Total	100.0	100.0	100.0	100.0	100.0
Number of cases	(12)	(151)	(207)	(17)	(68)

χ^2 = 874.5

Gamma = 0.85

TABLE 3.4   TRACK PLACEMENTS FOR NINTH AND TWELFTH GRADES

Twelfth Grade Track Placement	Ninth Grade Track Placement			
	College (%)	Upper Business (%)	Lower Business (%)	General (%)
Upper college	16.3	0.0	0.0	0.0
Lower college	54.3	0.0	0.0	0.0
Upper business	4.3	47.4	16.0	0.0
Lower business	5.4	36.8	44.0	55.6
Upper general	10.9	0.0	4.0	0.0
Lower general	8.7	15.8	36.0	44.1
Total	100.0	100.0	100.0	100.0
Number of cases	(92)	(19)	(25)	(9)

χ^2 = 109.1 with 15 df

Gamma = .66

college tracks, but 29% of the college track students move down into noncollege tracks. Indeed, the pattern of track change in the three-year interval is even more clear-cut than that in the one-year interval.

Although this research did not have access to school records for the first year of tracking (seventh grade), a small random sample of these students were asked about their track placements throughout junior and senior high school.[3] Table 3.5 shows students' reports of their seventh grade track and level placements compared with their twelfth grade track placements (taken from school records). One must be cautious in interpreting these data, both because of the small sample size and because the data are based on student recollections.[4] Yet even a cautious reading of this table shows definite patterns of track change, and they are the very same patterns observed previously. Most students in the two upper levels of the seventh grade language curriculum are in college tracks five years later. All students in the seventh grade nonlanguage curriculum are in the noncollege tracks five years later. Although many students move down in track (from upper to lower levels and from language to noncollege tracks), none move up. The student reports manifest considerable stability of track placements between seventh and twelfth grades, the only track changes being downward.

These results indicate that the seventh grade language and nonlanguage curricula have the same consequences as the college and noncollege tracks have in later years. The seventh grade language curriculum is a prerequisite for twelfth grade college track, and the upper levels of the language curriculum are a prerequisite for the upper college track. The lower levels of the language curriculum, like the lower college track, do not guarantee college track placement, and the selection process in the lower levels of the language curriculum is even more severe than in the lower college track. Thus, the language elective influences not only the entire seventh grade curriculum but also the track placement five years later. Although the college–noncollege terminology is not used in seventh grade, the language –nonlanguage distinction is its exact equivalent.

TABLE 3.5   TWELFTH GRADE TRACK PLACEMENT BY SEVENTH
GRADE CURRICULUM AND LEVEL PLACEMENT

Twelfth Grade Track Placement	Seventh Grade Curriculum and Level Placement		
	Language Curriculum Upper Levels	Language Curriculum Lower Levels	Nonlanguage Curriculum
Upper college	6	0	0
Lower college	10	4	0
Upper business	1	1	3
Lower business	1	1	3
Upper general	1	5	0
Lower general	1	10	3
Total	20	21	9

Although I have analyzed different kinds of data over different intervals, I have found similar patterns of change. In each of
these analyses I have found the same three processes:

1. There is virtually no change into or out of the upper college
   track.
2. There is virtually no change into college tracks from the noncollege tracks or the nonlanguage curriculum.
3. There is considerable change into noncollege tracks from the
   lower college track and the lower levels of the language curriculum.

Stability seems to be the chief characteristic of this system, and the
main opportunity for mobility is for downward change.[5]

Turner's Ideal Types Reconsidered.   Having described the norm,
stated policy, and actual social structure of the Grayton schools, I
am now in a position to reassess Turner's models. Grayton's
administrators support Turner's contention that the contest
model describes American norms. But the preceding analysis
does not support Turner's suggestion that the contest model

might describe the actual pattern of mobility. Although this model might be said to describe the lower college track, the sponsored model describes the upper college track and the noncollege tracks. Thus, the Grayton track system might be conceived as a combination of the sponsored and the contest models.

Actually, even this is an inadequate description. Turner's sponsorship posits a system where there is no mobility, and although there is no mobility out of the noncollege tracks, there is considerable movement into them. Turner's contest posits a system where there are no restrictions on mobility; yet Grayton's mobility is restricted to lower-college-track students. Furthermore, even they cannot compete for the upper college track; they can compete only to preserve their current status, and if they lose, they cannot compete again. In addition, lower-college-track students do not compete equally, for they are stratified into levels within that track. Thus, neither of Turner's ideal types is an adequate description of these tracks. Only the small upper college track fits one of Turner's ideal types exactly; it clearly fits the sponsored model.

Tournament Selection.   Turner's contest allows complete freedom for mobility, but his sponsorship allows no opportunity for mobility after selection. The Grayton track system resembles neither the contest nor the sponsored mobility ideal types. A far better metaphor for this track system is a tournament. The rule for tournament selection can be simply specified—*when you win, you win only the right to go on to the next round; when you lose, you lose forever.* The lower college track is the locus of the jousts, and each year a few more students are dropped from the competition. The openness in this system is like a valve that opens only downward. For those who win, the tournament promises the possibility of future successes. For those dropped, the tournament is over. No amount of striving can retrieve college track status once it is lost, and there are no playoffs among the losers.[6]

The tournament metaphor is not an ideal type like Turner's contest and sponsorship models. It describes actual practice, and it is not considered ideal. Tournament selection has two distinctive attributes. First, it creates a process of continual selection; each year selection shifts some students out of the college tracks. Second, it works in only one direction: students are eliminated from college tracks, but they never enter them.

Generalizability and the Coleman Discrepancy. The Coleman Report's simple question about the incidence of tracking elicited principals' reports which contradicted those by teachers and students. Furthermore, the contradiction is decidedly one directional. A majority of teachers report that tracking does exist in more than 80% of the schools that principals claim are untracked, but the opposite discrepancy is rare (Jencks, 1972, p. 453). This suggests that teachers are more likely to discern or report tracking than principals are, but it does not tell us which report is accurate or why the discrepancy occurs.

The data in my case study provide some clues here. We have seen that school administrators present a stated policy discrepant from the actual opportunity structure. They claim the school operates like the contest ideal type, but in fact, it has closed opportunities for many students. My observations suggest that Coleman's survey of administrators revealed their normative beliefs and stated policy—not the actual school structure.

The inconsistencies in the Coleman survey data suggest that we *cannot* learn about the generality of actual track structures by survey methods. Since administrators are the only individuals in a position to be aware of the entire track structure and since they are unwilling to divulge this information, we can learn about track structures only by more case studies such as this one.[7]

Of course, we do have a gross indication of whether tracking actually exists in a school by looking at the responses of a majority of its teachers. Ironically, although the disagreement between administrators and teachers in Coleman's survey prevents us from knowing how typical the Grayton track structure is, this disagreement does suggest that Grayton's discrepancy between policy and practice is typical!

One other case study has investigated selection practices, and it supports my conclusions. Cicourel and Kitsuse (1963) found that high school guidance counselors are extremely effective at limiting students' access to colleges, even against the pressures of upper-middle-class parents. Their results are particularly supportive of mine because they rely on different methods (observations of guidance counselors) in a very different kind of community (an upper-middle-class suburb). Thus, two schools in different communities have similar opportunity structures that minimize upward mobility.[8]

Although the differences between these two studies make them particularly compelling, two case studies do not prove that track systems always prevent upward mobility. The Coleman Report suggests that administrative deception is widespread, and that may lead us to suspect that administrators have something to hide about tracking. Furthermore, the next section offers reasons why many schools would be likely to encourage downward mobility and to restrict upward mobility. Yet the Coleman survey implies that we can learn of the generality of such practices only on a case-by-case basis. This inference must temper the enthusiasm for generalization, and it has important implications for policy making (cf. Chapter 10).

Reasons for a Tournament Structure.   The fact that so many administrators in the Coleman survey conceal the practice of tracking is striking. Even more striking is the extent to which the Grayton track structure deviates from the stated policy. We have every reason to believe that the Grayton administrators sincerely want to do a good job and offer the best education possible. Why, then, do they implement the tournament structure, which is so different from the contest policy?

Of course, the administrators would not say why they do so, but their interviews did give some indication of their reasons. Grayton administrators express a strong interest in economical use of school resources (such as science equipment, new textbooks, and well-qualified faculty), which they believe are in short supply, and they feel they must allocate them as efficiently as possible.

Grayton administrators also express a strong preoccupation with efficient use of time and training. They feel that students are better off choosing their careers early so that they will receive maximum preparation. They say that students are permitted to delay their decisions if they so choose, but the administrators believe this leads to wasted time in receiving preparation that may not be useful.

Moreover, Grayton administrators believe they can make reliable early selections of the students best qualified for higher education. The head guidance counselor assured me that the junior high counselors can predict who will do well in high school, who will not do well, who will drop out, and who will not even make it through junior high. He went on to add:

> In fact, I'm trying to look back to elementary school in making predictions of who will succeed and who will be the kids with problems. I think you can tell. I've noticed that the kid with good and bad grades tends to be smart but emotionally disturbed, and he will drop out of school on his sixteenth birthday [as soon as the law permits].

On another day, another counselor noted,

> The Protestant ethic is wrong. Hard work doesn't lead to success if you have low ability. A boy who is 5'2" can't be center on a basketball team. There is a real consistency from first grade to the end. It depends on a kid's native intelligence, what he thinks of himself, and how he reacts to school. Those things don't change.

Clearly, the guidance personnel do not feel any constraints about making an early judgment. They are confident about predicting a student's school career before he has finished the sixth grade.

In spite of their officially stated commitment to the contest norm, the Grayton administrators also hold beliefs implying that a late decision is needlessly inefficient. They believe that reliable

early predictions can be made effectively and that their implementation would lead to important efficiencies for the school
and for students in all tracks. These administrators are not alone
in their belief in efficiency; it is a pervasive norm throughout the
United States. Beliefs in the scarcity of school resources, the
efficiency of early preparation, and the predictability of contest
winners are widely held throughout American society.

This demand for efficiency tends to undermine the contest
norm. The contest norm encourages us to believe that selection
can continually be postponed (or even reversed) and that all
contestants enter each new competition with equal opportunities
for success. But efficiency undermines this process, encouraging
past performance to color later judgments. Thus the demand for
efficiency creates expectancy effects (Rosenthal and Jacobson,
1968) and social labeling processes (Schur, 1971) that make an
individual's history of successes and failures affect his access to
later competitions.

This argument may be extended one step further by a preview
of later findings. The risk of a contest's being undermined is
particularly great when personal histories are officially institutionalized into social categories like tracks. The lower tracks
are likely to receive quantitatively less and qualitatively different
instruction than upper tracks (Chapter 9). Even the best students
in a lower track will be deprived of the instruction offered to
upper-track students. Thus, in matching instruction and status to
past performance, a track system may guarantee that the losers in
a competition—even those who are misplaced—are never again
in a position to compete with past winners (Chapter 7). Even
incorrect track placements would tend to be self-perpetuating. If
this line of reasoning is correct, then the lack of upward track
changes in Grayton is likely to be widespread in track systems.

In the context of these processes, the tournament emerges as a
natural substitute for the contest model. Society expects schools
to promote opportunity according to the contest norm, but society also expects the efficiency of early selection. The two expectations are diametrically opposed, and neither a contest nor a

sponsorship can satisfy them. The tournament can be seen as a natural consequence of this conflict. The continual selection of the tournament suggests that opportunity has not been completely closed. Consequently, the tournament encourages competition and postpones ultimate selection and thereby demands continual striving from the (lower college track) elite. Those retaining elite status must work at it—they cannot slip into an aristocratic demeanor. On the other hand, the impossibility of upward mobility in the tournament permits the efficiency of a sponsorship by allowing "time to prepare the masses. . .to accept their inferiority and to make 'realistic' rather than fantasy plans" (Turner, 1960, p. 858). The desire to maintain the appearance of a contest while simultaneously introducing efficient selections makes the tournament an extremely likely solution.

Of course, the tournament appears to reconcile values that are ultimately irreconcilable. It encourages students to accept the stated contest policy as a faithful description of the real situation. But while fostering the illusion of a contest, it condemns some students to low-status positions offering no opportunity. It also provides efficiency in socializing students into their respective positions as if it were a sponsorship, but the discontent generated by continual downward mobility threatens the system's stability. The tournament does not reconcile the conflicting values of opportunity and efficiency—as evidenced by the administrators' need to maintain a deceptive stated policy—but it does provide the illusion of reconciliation, which may serve a legitimizing function.

Conclusions and Implications.   The task of this chapter has been the extension of recent work by Coleman and Jencks, to understand the operation of educational selection within schools, to unravel a contradiction in the Coleman Report, and to discover the relevance of Turner's ideal types. It was found that, even in a socially homogeneous, comprehensive high school where the contest norm is most likely to be implemented and where it is indeed the stated policy, the actual structure severely restricts opportunity. Because track placements are unrelated to any (measurable) social class variables, this closed opportunity structure cannot be attributed to social discrimination; it is the result of tracking per se. The concept of tracking has been shown to be likely to foster such a structure, and Cicourel and Kitsuse's study of tracking in a very different setting supports these findings. The contest norm is unlikely to describe the opportunity structure of American high schools.

These results do not contradict Turner, for he clearly states that "the ideal types are not fully exemplified in practice" (*ibid.*, p. 856). His contention is that the contest norm is a guiding force on policy and practice, and the Grayton student handbook and the administrators' statements support him. That the Grayton administrators continue to affirm the contest norm while implementing a closed opportunity structure demonstrates just how important the contest norm is.

Yet my analyses extend and elaborate Turner's analysis. This study notes that the fundamental value conflict between opportunity and efficiency to which Turner alludes can occur within a single school and can encourage divergences between stated policies and actual structures. The contradiction in the Coleman Report suggests that these deviations may be quite widespread, and my findings suggest that Coleman's survey of administrators revealed their normative beliefs but not the actual school structure. This study also notes that the actual opportunity structure can possess some attributes of both the contest and sponsored ideal types, and the tournament model employs a quasi-contest competition to continually eliminate students from the possibility of success. Finally, I have argued that the stated (contest) policy can have an important legitimizing function by delaying students' awareness of their actual lack of opportunities (cf. Chapter 6).

This is the first study to investigate the opportunity structure within a school. My discovery of tournament selection is likely to have important ramifications on many aspects of educational selection. If this selection results in early permanent placements within schools, then our customary nonchalance about selection criteria, college and job allocation, and the role of personal choice is no longer warranted, and these issues require investigation (see Chapters 4, 5, and 6). Furthermore, the rigidity of the tournament structure suggests not only that it responds to individual attributes as a selection system but also that it might socialize individuals differently who pass through this system (see Chapters 7, 8, and 9).

NOTES

1. Note that a few records were not complete, particularly for mathematics enrollment.

2. The high school records available to this research varied in the number of categories exhibited (5 for tenth grade, 4 for ninth). Because the ninth grade records were made available to the researcher for only a limited time, only a one-third random sample was taken.

3. This sample and the interview are described in the Appendix to Chapter 2.

4. One might suspect that student recollections might be distorted to be consistent with current track placement. Although plausible, this seems unlikely for two reasons. First, the findings of this analysis are completely consistent with the preceding analyses of school records. Second, because level placements are associated with foreign language elective, we have a check on students' level recollections. Both students and administrators report that students are encouraged to take Latin and French if they are good students, and students taking these languages would be in the top two levels. Guidance counselors advise slower students that Latin and French are too hard for them, and such students are advised to take Italian and Spanish and are placed in lower levels. In the interviews, students' reports of their levels also noted their language course, and their reports of levels and lan-

guage were consistent. Although students could easily fail to remember the number of their level, it is unlikely that they would misremember the foreign language they took.

5. Even the small amount of upward mobility manifested in these tables can be explained by hidden aspects of tracking. In each of the three largest tracks, there are many classes, and the school ranks and classifies these classes into different sections. These sections not only multiply the number of levels within the track structure, but they also influence mobility between tracks. Thus, in the lower college track, 20% of the highest section and none of the other two sections move into the upper college track. Similar patterns are evident in the business and general tracks.

6. The assumption behind a tournament is that, if a person loses in an early competition, then he could never win in a later one. In tournaments, such as tennis tournaments, that select a single winner by pairwise competitions, the underlying assumption is the same as the mathematical assumption of transitivity, that is, if $a > b$ and $b > c$, then $a > c$. The problem with the tournament assumption is that it describes human performances only in a probabilistic way. The practice of allowing rematches and the uncertainties of gamblers' odds suggest that the tournament assumption is not a very reliable predictor of human performance.

7. This description suggests that surveys of school administrators, the most common means of studying school structure, will produce untrustworthy results. In contrast, surveys of students and teachers can provide useful information, but they are unlikely to have an understanding of the overall structure.

8. Cicourel and Kitsuse do not analyze the pattern of track placements, and so we cannot make more extensive comparisons.

Chapter 4   Meritocracy and Tracking

T he desire to match the best individuals with the highest
    social positions is not unique to Grayton. We all feel it would
be beneficial if the best people had the highest positions in society.
This vision has somehow eluded realization, but it has persistently
attracted people's hopes. Plato's *Republic* portrays such a dream,
tantalizing us with an image of society governed by the wisest
people and therefore productive, prosperous, stable, and secure.

Of course, the belief in better and worse people is not compati-
ble with the belief in equality; it implies that opportunity is harm-
ful to the common welfare. Plato conceived men to be born
possessing different worth, as if composed of different metals:
the rulers composed of gold, the auxiliaries of silver, and the
workers of brass and iron. Consequently, in his view, a society

Tape: 4a   Job No.: 516
Ms/c pages: chap 4 (56-92)

offering everyone self-advancement opportunities runs the risk of being dominated by opportunists with more ambition than ability. He avoided the risk of having leaders composed of base metal by establishing a rigid aristocracy—not the false aristocracy based on family status, but the true aristocracy of merit.

Plato's vision of the ideal state also goes beyond selection and places great stress on the early onset of appropriate education. According to Plato, if we want a society where the best people govern, then we must select the best people quite early, before they are tarnished by exposure to lesser sorts, and train them to acquire the skills, virtues, and temperament required for governing the state.

Much contemporary thinking about selection reflects Plato's ideas. British sociologist Michael Young (1958) coined the word *meritocracy* to describe a system matching social position with talent; like Plato, he argues that efficiency requires meritocracy:

> Social progress depends upon the degree to which power is matched with . . . [talent. A society] squanders its resources by condemning . . . talented people to ordinary education and manual work (*ibid.*, p. 14).

Sociological theory (Davis and Moore, 1945; Turner, 1960) and recent popular articles (e.g., Herrnstein, 1971) argue that efficiency requires the restriction of opportunity. We recall that Turner's sponsored ideal type strives for the same goal as Plato's *Republic:* "to make the best use of talents in society by sorting each person into his proper niche." And like Plato's *Republic*, Turner's sponsorship stresses the role of schools in creating the efficient society: "Early selection allows time to prepare the recruits for their elite position" and to socialize "the masses . . . to accept their inferiority" (Turner, 1960).

As offensive as this argument sounds to our democratic ears, it seems to have a compelling logic behind it. Society would undoubtedly be more productive, stable, and secure if it were governed by its most talented citizens. Are we not, therefore, bound to join Plato and the others in advocating an aristocracy of merit?

Rather than condemn the Grayton track system because it precludes opportunity for most students, should we not appreciate that tracking performs a vital selection function, contributing to the productivity and welfare of society by discovering the most talented youth?

Empirical Issues Underlying Meritocratic Selection.   If selections are not to be arbitrary, they must be based on an appropriate criterion, and the choice of an appropriate criterion is a fundamental problem for any selection system. Traditional societies based selections on social origins, but, once we have rejected that, we must search for another criterion. A nineteenth-century utopian community, Oneida, implemented a eugenics system allowing only the most nearly perfect males to father children, and they trusted their charismatic leader's judgments about who was nearly enough perfect to reproduce. Not surprisingly, their leader fathered most children born to the community, and when members began to question his judgment, their perfectionist experiment came to an end (Carden, 1969). Evidently, a selection system based on a charismatic leader's judgment is a fragile arrangement.

Plato must have been aware of the dilemma of choosing an appropriate selection criterion, but he avoided discussing it. His myth of men of different metals justifies selection without providing guidelines for selecting the men made of gold.

Michael Young describes a system based on an objective criterion, but his account itself reflects the problem of choosing a selection criterion. He says the criterion is intelligence, but then he waffles in his definition of intelligence, at first suggesting it is academic ability (as in our current IQ tests) and later defining it in terms of generalized job skills. Young's explicit definition of intelligence emerges near the end of his book: "the ability to raise production, directly or indirectly" *ibid.,* p. 168). This definition establishes the importance of intelligence for a productive society tautologically, but it does not tell us what intelligence is. It is hard to conceive what general ability underlies the productivity of plumbers, painters, politicians, and physicists. Young confuses the issue further when he momentarily realizes the limitations of intelligence and feels compelled to add that "effort" is an important component of the selection criterion (*ibid.*, p. 94). His attempt illustrates the difficulty of choosing a criterion.

Ever since Plato, philosophers have argued about the best qualities for leaders to possess, and these issues cannot be resolved here. But even putting these issues aside, there are practical requirements which place important constraints on what selection criterion is chosen and how it is used. Of course, practical requirements do not tell us which indicators measure merit, for that is a question of values, but they can tell us which indicators are not appropriate for meritocratic selection. These practical requirements can be investigated by empirical methods, and such an empirical analysis can reveal some of the constraints on the possibility of meritocratic selection.

The theoretical justification of meritocracy poses three practical requirements. If meritocratic selection restricts opportunity for the sake of efficiency, then the criterion must have certain characteristics and be applied in certain ways to ensure its efficiency. Permanent selections can be efficient only if they are based on a *valid* and *stable* criterion. If the criterion is not a valid measure of the merit attribute or if it is unstable, then the permanent placements would not be efficient over time. Furthermore, selections must also be *completely based on the criterion.* Any departure from the criterion for the selection of particular individuals undermines the efficiency justification of the selection process.

These same three requirements are also supported by the "due process" provision in the U.S. Constitution. Although the requirements of "due process" are not entirely clear when applied to selection within schools (Kirp, 1973), due process has been legally interpreted to require at a minimum that a selection criterion be reasonably valid and stable *(Griggs* v. *Duke Power Co.)* and that it be applied to all students in the same way *(Smuck* v. *Hobson).* Both theoretical and legal justifications for meritocratic selection assume, therefore, that selection criteria are valid, stable, and applied to everyone in the same way. Empirical analysis can investigate whether these assumptions are warranted in particular selection systems.

As social theorists from Plato to Turner have noted, the most important selection system in a meritocratic society is in the schools, for schools are the most appropriate institutions for executing social selection and socialization. A school is run by and for the society, and, hence, it may implement any kind of selection the society considers desirable. Because the school's curriculum represents the skills, knowledge, and values considered essential to the society's welfare, a student's ability to master this curriculum represents an ideal test of his capacity to take responsibility in society. Furthermore, school teachers are professionals specially trained in this curriculum; consequently, they make particularly effective agents for performing society's selection process.

Because of school's importance in creating a meritocratic society, the study of a school track system provides an excellent opportunity to investigate the practical constraints on meritocratic selection. Some proponents of tracking claim that its purpose is to advance meritocratic aims (Hansen, 1964). The channeling of opportunities discovered in Grayton and the administrators' concern with early detection of ability suggest that the track system is intended to execute meritocratic selection. A school track system is, moreover, a particularly good setting to investigate the use of criteria in meritocracy, because a school provides many evaluative indices of merit. This chapter attempts to discover some of the constraints on the possibility of meritocratic selection by analyzing three aspects of Grayton's selections:

1. Are potential selection criteria valid and stable?
2. Are selection criteria applied to everyone in the same way?
3. How do selection criteria define the selection system?

American Norms for Merit Criteria.   Meritocratic selection strikes a responsive chord in the American value system. There is nothing more clear about American norms than that ancestry is not valued as a criterion of selection. American folklore is replete with stories emphasizing "rags to riches" selection. In stories of competition between a person privileged by birth and a lowly born person of merit, every child knows not to place his bets on the well born.

American norms are not, however, clear about the particular criterion that might be used for meritocratic selection. In various contexts, different qualities, such as ability, effort, and achievement, seem to be considered meritorious, but no quality seems to enjoy unqualified endorsement.

Ability is certainly the first quality one thinks of as a criterion of merit, and yet American norms show an ambivalence toward talent (Hofstadter, 1962). Ivory-tower intellectuals are considered irrelevant or impotent by the businessman and his agents. Even within schools, "brains," as well as "underachievers," are said to be unsuited to selection for high social position (Coleman, 1961).

Effort as a criterion of merit harks back to the Calvinistic tradition, and success, like redemption, derives therefrom (Weber, 1958). Appeals to "hard work" have often been the fuel of conservative populist movements, and even liberals have used such appeals to condemn "the indolent rich." Even a famous American inventor (Edison) attributed his genius to effort: "genius is 1% inspiration and 99% perspiration." Yet in society and in the schools, effort is not sufficient to be considered as merit. People who strive very hard but who lack ability are considered "overachievers," and, though they may gain some positive regard, this is not respect, and the awards of high esteem are generally withheld.

Achievement is often used as a practical definition of ability and effort, because these two qualities are hard to judge. As such it follows the same positivist epistemology as Skinnerian psychology: a person is like a "black box"; one cannot know what qualities are inside, but he must have some very good qualities if he has many achievements. Of course, one cannot be sure that only ability and effort were involved in an achievement. Craftiness, deception, corruption, or just plain luck have also been known to be involved. Given that some less-than-meritorious qualities are inside the "black box," achievement may be viewed cynically as a criterion of merit.

Clearly then, although American norms unequivocally reject ancestry as a criterion of merit, they are ambiguous about what criteria are important. Within education, the conflict has been particularly acute.

> There has always been a conflict in American education between the idea that academic credentials should measure competence and the idea that they should reward effort. The result has been a series of battles between those who want to maintain standards by failing students who do poor work and those who want to encourage academic effort by conferring diplomas and degrees on people who have tried to do academic work, regardless of whether they did it well or poorly (Jencks, 1972, p. 143).

Given the ambiguity and conflicts among norms, it is hard to predict which criterion a school would select to reflect merit.

Merit Criteria in School Records.   As if to ratify the preceding norms, most schools keep exhaustive records of precisely those student characteristics just discussed. Student ability, effort, and achievement are recorded and preserved for evaluation and selection.

The Grayton school system places considerable importance on the completeness of its records, and teachers report that a single omission on the daily attendance record brings far stronger rebuke from the administration than complaints about the quality of one's teaching.[1] An examination of the school records found them extraordinarily complete, and comparisons with raw data, when possible, found them quite accurately recorded. The records provide several indicators of ability and effort, both objective and subjective. There is also an indicator of achievement.

The following are the indicators available in Grayton's school records:

ABILITY

Objective Indicators.   IQ scores (Otis–Lennon) and verbal and mathematical aptitude scores (School and College Ability Test —SCAT) are commonly used as standardized and objective indicators of ability. Grayton administered these tests in eighth and tenth grades to all students in the school system.

Subjective Indicators.   Grayton ninth grade teachers submit a numerical evaluation of each student's potential for high school. Although subjective, this rating had the value of being based on actual behavior in the classroom over an entire year.

EFFORT

Objective Indicator.   The school keeps good records of each student's daily attendance. Given the importance the administrators place on accurate recordkeeping, the attendance record is likely to be an objective indicator of a minimal level of effort. "The student who has spent 12 years in attendance is generally felt to have earned some kind of diploma, and it seems unfair to send him away empty handed" (Jencks et al., 1972, p. 144).

Subjective Indicators.   Teachers evaluate students on industry and deportment (on a four-point scale) for every course they take. These are subjective evaluations, and yet idiosyncratic aspects are canceled out by averaging different teachers' ratings. Although this makes these ratings more reliable, it does not make them any the less subjective. Averaged ratings are based on any common values that the teachers in the school might employ.

These values might be valid for judging the student's effort, or they might be irrelevant and discriminatory (e.g., based on a student's speech accent, quality of dress, or personal habits; see Rist, 1970).

ACHIEVEMENT

Subjective Indicator   Each student is given an achievement grade for each course. Like the subjective indicators of effort, grades are subject to the same kinds of collective biases, but averaging of grades minimizes idiosyncratic biases of individual teachers.

Testing The Three Assumptions of Meritocratic Tracking   A meritocratic system is based on three tacit assumptions: that the selection criterion is valid, that it is stable, and that the system operates universalistically (the same way toward everybody) on the basis of this criterion. Since a meritocracy makes early permanent selections, these three assumptions are crucial to the justification of meritocratic selection. This section investigates whether any of the potential criteria in the Grayton school records might have the right characteristics and be appropriately applied to make the Grayton track system meritocratic.

1. *Are the potential selection criteria valid?*

Before we use a measuring instrument for selecting people for privileged positions, we would like to be confident that it actually measures real differences among people: that is, that it makes "valid" distinctions. Social researchers define validity as "the extent to which differences in scores on (the measuring instrument) reflect true differences among individuals . . ." (Selltiz et al., 1962, p. 155). One test for the validity of an indicator is whether other indicators of the same attribute are highly related to the first indicator. If there is not substantial correlation among different indicators of the same attribute, then one must doubt that these indicators are actually measuring the same underlying attribute.

The Grayton school records provide four indicators of ability: three tests (IQ, SCAT Verbal, and SCAT Mathematics) and one teacher rating. The correlations among these are all quite high (see Table 4.1).[2] For example, if a student has a high SCAT Verbal score, one could be confident that he would have high scores on his other ability tests. These correlations suggest that all the indicators of ability are tapping the same underlying attribute and that each might be considered a valid indicator of ability.

The correlations among the three effort indicators (industry, deportment, attendance) are not very large. For instance, attendance is related to industry, but only modestly, and it is not at all related to deportment. In other words, those individuals showing high effort in terms of attendance do not necessarily show high effort in terms of industry or deportment. If individuals differ in the effort they exert in school, this difference is not consistently measured by all the indicators that would be expected to reflect effort. One cannot, therefore, have much confidence that any of these indicators is a valid measure of an underlying personal attribute, and one could not be comfortable about basing permanent selections on any of them.

Grade point average (GPA) is the only indicator the school records offer for achievement. The correlation between grades and industry is very large, nearly half the variation of grades being explained by industry. The correlations of grades with the ability tests are not nearly so large. More detailed analyses (using regression procedures) indicate that, if we let industry explain as much of grades as it can, then ability test scores can explain only a negligible amount of the remaining variation (2%), but industry explains a great deal after ability (27%). These correlations suggest that industry and grades measure the same attribute in students. We cannot, therefore, consider grades to reflect an attribute that is much different than industry, and we must conclude that we have no independent indicator for achievement.[3]

TABLE 4.1. CORRELATIONS AMONG INDICATORS OF ABILITY, EFFORT, AND ACHIEVEMENT

Indicator	IQ	SCAT Verbal	SCAT Math	Rating	Industry	Deportment	Attendance
Ability							
IQ	1.00						
SCAT verbal	.72	1.00					
SCAT math	.70	.95	1.00				
Rating	.57	.53	.51	1.00			
Effort							
Industry	.39	.44	.42	.42	1.00		
Deportment	.13	.15	.14	.22	.46	1.00	
Attendance	.13	.26	.25	.17	.30	.08	1.00
Achievement							
GPA	.44	.44	.40	.39	.67	.30	.35

The preceding analysis demonstrates that the various indicators of effort have insufficient intercorrelations to justify considering them as valid measures of a real personal attribute, and we could not be comfortable about basing permanent selections on any of these indicators. Nor were our expectations about achievement borne out, for grades are so highly related to industry as to suggest that they are not an independent indicator for achievement. The correlations do, however, suggest that the ability indicators may be considered to be valid measures of a real personal trait.[4]

2.   Are potential selection criteria stable?

The efficiency of a meritocracy comes from its early selection of people to receive appropriate training for their future careers. But a meritocracy can be efficient only if it is based on a stable selection criterion. If a criterion were unstable, then the training provided at any particular time would be inappropriate a short time later.

Research suggests that IQ scores are very stable after the age of nine, Bloom (1964, p. 64) reporting that IQ scores are nearly as stable in the 9–17 age span as the test is reliable on two testings at age 17 (.90 correlation for the Stanford–Binet). Studies of school grades suggest less stability, but even here, the stability is considerable—all the studies reported by Bloom report correlations of more than .60 (ibid., p. 98). These results, and the studies of intellectual motivation in laboratory situations, point to considerable stability of effort (most correlations more than .60; ibid., p. 144). The conclusion to be drawn from the multitude of studies that Bloom presents is that these indicators are all quite stable for at least the eight-year period after the age of nine. Any indicator would, therefore, be an adequately stable selection criterion, and IQ would be ideal.

The high school records provide repeated measures for the IQ and SCAT tests in eighth and tenth grades and for all other indicators (except teachers' rating) between tenth and twelfth grades. The records available to this research permit analysis of stability over only a two-year interval. Therefore, it is all the more striking that, despite the fact that these indicators are taken at an older age and over a shorter interval than those in the studies reported by Bloom, all indicators show much lower stability in this study than in the studies reported by Bloom (see Table 4.2).

TABLE 4.2. STABILITY CORRELATIONS OVER
A TWO-YEAR INTERVAL

IQ	SCAT Verbal	SCAT Math	Industry	Deportment	Attendance	Grades
.63	.65	.53	.48	.32	.36	.47

Despite the findings reported by Bloom, we conclude that the indicators in this school are not very stable: the effort indicators predict less than 25% of the variance of their later scores, and the ability indicators predict about 40%.[5] Clearly, the effort measures are not sufficiently stable to be used in selecting students for permanent meritocratic positions, and the ability measures, though better, have great risks of misplacement.

3. *Is the selection criterion applied to everyone in the same way?*

Meritocracy demands that talent not be squandered by allocation to low positions and that performance not be impaired by distribution of students with low talent to highly demanding positions. The concept of meritocracy assumes that the selection criterion actually measures a person's suitability for a position. In other words, there is a range on the selection criterion that marks the level of merit required for the position, and all those in the range should be in the position and all those outside the range should not be in that position. Meritocracy demands, therefore, that track placements be universalistic; that is, that the criteria be applied to everyone in the same way.

Universalistic selection means that, if 37% of the students in our twelfth grade sample are in the college track and IQ is the sole selection criterion, then the college track should comprise virtually all students who scored in the top 37% of the IQ test, that is, those with IQ greater than 106. If grade point average (GPA) is the sole criterion, and the top 37% have an average better than 2.49 (B-), then that would be the cutoff point for college track. Such cutoff points are arbitrary, but they can be made.

On the other hand, industry is not a continuous variable; it just has four different values. Since the teachers themselves place students in these categories, the distinctions between these categories have some significance to teachers and are not so arbitrary. But the distinctions are not at the right place, for industry does not provide a 37% cutoff point (16% of the students received the top rating in industry and 62% received the top two ratings).

In an ideal meritocracy, the selection criterion would combine the advantages of each of these: there would be a discrete cutoff point on the criterion scale where there were few scores requiring arbitrary track assignments, and this point would correspond to the level of merit required for the upper tracks. For a discrete scale like industry, this requires the discrete categories to come in the right part of the scale; for example, 37% of students would be rated in the top two categories of industry. For a continuous scale like IQ, the ideal requires a bimodal distribution, with nearly all students at the two ends of the scale and relatively few individuals at the cutoff point. The indicators in the school records do not satisfy these conditions. The discrete scale indicators have the breaks at the wrong places, and the continuous scale indicators have their cutoff points in the most populous part of their distribution. The indicators in the school records are not, therefore, distributed in such a way as to facilitate an ideal meritocracy.

Table 4.3 shows the proportion of students in college-track placements for each percentile range of the school record indicators.[6] Ideally, the first two ranges would be entirely college-track students, and the last two would be entirely noncollege-track students. Although this table demonstrates that` track placement is highly, and significantly, related to all indicators, no scale has a perfect correspondence with track placement, even in the top and bottom intervals. Even students scoring in the top 12% of these scales are not guaranteed college-track placement. From 10% to 26% of students in the top 12% interval

TABLE 4.3. PROPORTION OF STUDENTS IN COLLEGE-TRACK PLACEMENTS FOR EACH PERCENTILE RANGE OF THE SCHOOL RECORD INDICATORS

Indicator	Highest 100–88%	87–65%	65–15%	Lowest 14–0%	n
IQ	87.0	52.6	26.2	5.0	184
Teacher's recommendation	88.2	55.9	36.1	5.9	151
Grade point average	73.9	57.1	32.2	2.9	189
Attendance	82.6	53.5	23.7	27.8	181
Industry	Highest 16% 83.9	Highest 72% 41.4	Lowest 37% 14.8	Lowest 5% 0.0	189
Deportment	Highest 79% 43.3	Lowest 21% 20.0	Lowest 5% 0.0	Lowest 1% 0.0	189

of these scales are not in the college track. The lowest intervals of most scales correspond more closely to track placement; yet, even in the lowest 14% of most scales, there are many college-track students.[7]

Of course, one cannot be certain that track placements are based on a single criterion. Because of the instability of indicators, the school might have used a combination of two or more indicators to determine track placement. In a painstaking investigation, I was unable to find any combination of these indicators that universalistically explains track placements or track changes, even at the ends of the scales (see Rosenbaum, 1973). For example, a comprehensive factor was constructed of the sum of IQ, teacher's ability rating, industry, and attendance, and this factor was compared with college-track placement (see Table 4.4). Although this factor has the closest correspondence with placement of all factors investigated (all students in the top 14% are in college tracks and all in the bottom 5% are in noncollege tracks), the relationship rapidly deteriorates, even in the next 10%, where more than a quarter of the best students are in noncollege tracks. Although track placements may be highly related to some combination of criteria at the very top and bottom of the scale, this explains very few placements, and nonuniversalistic placement still exists for the middle 80%. Hence, track selection appears quite unsystematic.

IQ as a Criterion over Time.   In the foregoing, I was concerned only with judging whether school record indicators are universalistically applied in assigning track placements. This section examines the deviations from universalistic placement to determine where and when the track system permits exceptions to the meritocratic standard.

I have chosen to examine the relationship between track placement and IQ. IQ has several characteristics that make detailed examination of its relationship to track placement particularly significant. It is a standardized, objective, and relatively stable score. Thus, not only can one consider IQ scores to be reasonably reliable and valid, but one can also determine in what intervals of the IQ scale selection decisions can be made with

TABLE 4.4. TRACK BY COMPREHENSIVE FACTOR (THE SUM OF IQ, TEACHER'S ABILITY RATING, INDUSTRY, AND ATTENDANCE)

	Comprehensive Factor*								
Track	High All Criteria (Highest 8%) 6	(Highest 13%) 7	(Highest 24%) 8	(Highest 32%) 9	(Highest 49%) 10	(Lowest 51%) 11	(Lowest 30%) 12	(Lowest 13%) 13	Low All Criteria (Lowest 5%) 14
College track	100.0	100.0	73.7	46.2	33.3	27.8	6.5	13.3	0.0
Noncollege track	0.0	0.0	26.3	53.8	66.7	72.2	93.5	86.7	100.0
Total	100.0	100.0	100.0	100.0	100.0	100.0	100.0	100.0	100.0
Number of cases	(15)	(9)	(19)	(13)	(30)	(36)	(31)	(15)	(9)

χ^2 = 73.8 with 8 df

Gamma = 0.77

*The comprehensive factor is the sum of IQ, teacher's ability rating, industry, and attendance. Before this factor was computed, IQ and attendance were coded into four categories, whose distribution was similar to the distribution of teacher's ability rating (see Table 4.3).

confidence. The standard error for the Otis IQ test is four points. "In other words, the 'true score' of one child in twenty is likely to depart from his obtained score by more than plus or minus eight points of standardized score" (Yates, 1966, p. 499). If IQ = 106 is used as the cutoff point for college-track placement (the point where 37% of the students are above that score), then students scoring 114 are unlikely (probability less than 2½%) to have "true scores" at or below the cutoff, and students scoring below 99 are unlikely to have "true scores" above the cutoff. In a meritocratic track system based on IQ, we can be confident about the track placements of students above and below the 99–114 interval. All scores above this interval clearly belong in the college track, and all below it belong in noncollege tracks. We can make no confident decisions about scores within the central interval; therefore, the administrators might choose to include or exclude all students in this interval or to apply another criterion.

Figure 4.1 graphs the percent of ninth grade students in the college track by IQ for the entire class of 1971 ($n = 457$). This graph bears some resemblance to the model of meritocracy just discussed. Since a steep slope signifies that a high degree of differentiation is being made in an interval, this graph shows that ninth grade school policy treats those just beyond the central interval very differently than those within the interval. Those just

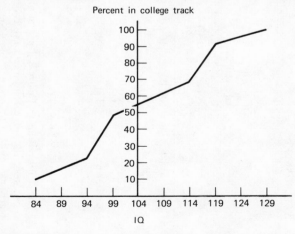

Figure 4.1.   IQ by percent of students in the college track in ninth grade.

above this interval are largely guaranteed college-track placement and those just below it are more likely to be excluded. Yet
for the most part, this graph demonstrates that the ninth grade
track system is rather inclusive, giving the benefit of a doubt to
students in the questionable region. Half to three-quarters of
students in the central interval are placed in college track, and
nearly half the students just below the lower cutoff point are in
college track. Thus, ninth grade track placement operates like a
meritocracy only in the upper interval; in the middle and lower
intervals there is a tendency to give students the benefit of a doubt
in spite of low scores.

Track placement in tenth and twelfth grades is quite different.
Figure 4.2 portrays the relationship of IQ to track placement in
ninth, tenth, and twelfth grades. In contrast to the inclusive
pattern in ninth grade, track placements in tenth and twelfth
grades are quite exclusive, giving the benefit of a doubt to few
students. At every part of the IQ scale, with the exception of the
top and bottom 2%, the percentage of students in college tracks is
considerably less in the later years. All students in the top 2% of
IQ are in college track in the twelfth grade, but the percentage
falls off rapidly below that. In the next five-point interval (in the
top 7%) more than one-fifth are in noncollege tracks, and in the
following five-point interval (in the top 16%) more than two-fifths
are in noncollege tracks. Thus, in contrast to ninth grade track
placement, twelfth grade had no point of guarantee of college-
track placement short of the very top of the scale (the top 2%).
The upper interval is not a plateau, as in ninth grade, but is a
steep slope, illustrating differentiation along the whole upper
interval. Indeed, this small interval (the top quarter of the IQ
scale) is the interval where most of the differentiation does occur.
At the bottom of the upper interval (e.g., 114–119), only one-
third of the students are in the college track. Thereafter, the
chances decrease further, but more slowly, for only one-third of
the differentiation remains for the bottom three-quarters of the
scale.

The ninth grade track placement curve suggests a tendency to
include students in college track if there is any chance that they

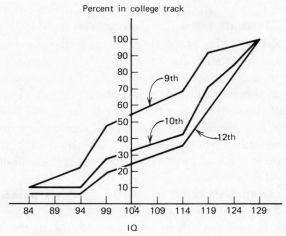

Figure 4.2.   IQ by percent of students in the college track in ninth, tenth, and twelfth grades.

are able to do the work, but the twelfth grade curve exhibits a tendency to exclude students if there is any chance that they are not able to do the work. Neither is completely meritocratic. The ninth grade track system is meritocratic in the upper interval, but it allows too many low-IQ students into college track to be considered meritocratic. The twelfth grade track system is meritocratic in excluding low-IQ students from college track, but it excludes too many high-IQ students to be considered meritocratic. Obviously, if one is concerned about the risk of excluding talented students, it is preferable to have an inclusive system that errs toward giving students the benefit of a doubt. Yet a system that does not apply its selection criterion in the same way for everybody implies that the criterion has no intrinsic relationship to track placements. It means that low-IQ students can do college track work, and this undermines the significance of the criterion and the selection process. Neither the inclusive pattern of ninth grade nor the exclusive pattern of twelfth grade offers students a rational justification for their track position.

This track system changes dramatically in the three years between ninth and twelfth grade, from an inclusive to an exclusive system. During the course of high school a severe weeding-out process occurs, directed at all parts of the IQ scale and eliminating nearly all students in the lower interval, most in the central interval, and many in the upper interval. Since all but the top 2% are vulnerable to downward mobility, the process leads to a considerable loss of talent and to indiscriminate selections at all portions of the IQ scale.

The Relative Influence of Ability and Effort. Although school record criteria are not categorically related to track placements, they are highly related. These school record indicators may have considerable bearing on track placements. We have seen that IQ, attendance, and teachers' ratings of ability and industry are all related to track placements, even though none is applied universalistically. The statistical procedure of regression permits us to analyze how much of the variation in track placement can be explained by all these criteria combined. Furthermore, it allows us to sort out the separate influences of the different factors.

Generally, in regression analyses, we do not expect to be able to explain all the variance; yet there are several reasons for expecting that this might be possible here. The main reason is that we have all the potential criteria the school could reasonably use for selections. The guidance counselors are the actual agents influencing selections, but, given the large number of students each counselor must deal with (450), these counselors can only make knowledgeable judgements based on the official school criteria. Insofar as the counselors' selection decisions (based on their brief exposure to students) are different from teachers' evaluations (based on a yearlong exposure to students), their selections will be questionable. Even a selection policy based on global evaluations rather than specific test scores would have most validity if it were based on the teachers' global ratings which exist in the school records, rather than on counselors' global evaluations. Thus it may well be expected that this analysis of the combined influence of school criteria might explain 100% of the variance of track placements.

Table 4.5 presents the results of the regression analysis of twelfth grade track placement (college vs. noncollege tracks) on

TABLE 4.5. REGRESSION OF COLLEGE TRACK ON ABILITY
AND EFFORT*

	Boys		Girls	
Criteria	Unique Variance (%)	Total Variance (%)	Unique Variance (%)	Total Variance (%)
Ability	11	28	5	12
Effort	15	32	15	22
Shared	17		7	
Total	43		27	

*Ability is composed of variance explained by IQ and teacher's recom-
mendations. Effort is composed of variance explained by industry and
attendance.

the most important school record indicators.[8,9,10] They are
grouped by the conceptual distinction used earlier—ability (IQ
and teacher's ability ratings) and effort (industry and attendance). Table 4.6 displays the comparable regressions for track
changes (between ninth and twelfth grades; for coding, see Appendix). These tables show that all the school criteria combined
do not explain even half of the variance of track placements or

TABLE 4.6. REGRESSION OF TRACK CHANGE ON ABILITY
AND EFFORT*

	Boys		Girls	
Criteria	Unique Variance (%)	Total Variance (%)	Unique Variance (%)	Total Variance (%)
Ability	4	14	2	5
Effort	18	28	6	8
Shared	10		2	
Total	32		10	

*Ability is composed of variance explained by IQ and teacher's recom-
mendations. Effort is composed of variance explained by industry and
attendance.

track changes. Conceivably, the school may use nonlinear or complex sequential selection procedures (which these regression equations do not analyze), but this seems improbable. My results suggest that most track placements cannot be explained by simple linear combinations of all the school record indicators.

Besides exhibiting the combined influence of the four school record indicators, these tables also manifest the separate influences of ability and effort. Since the ability indicators are correlated with the effort indicators, I want to sort out this shared component. To discern the separate influence of ability, independent of effort, we must see how much of the variation of track placement can be explained by ability after effort has explained all that it can explain. This is called the unique influence or the unique variance explained by ability. Similarly, the unique influence of effort is the amount of track variation that effort can explain after ability has explained all that it can. The two unique variances do not include the influence that comes from both ability and effort jointly. This is called the shared influence (or shared variance) of ability and effort. Thus, regression allows us to separate out the unique influence of ability, the unique influence of effort, and the shared influence of the two. For determining the relative influence of ability and effort, their unique influences are compared.

We must recall that ability and effort indicators are not equally appropriate for making track selections. The ability indicators are relatively stable, but the effort indicators are not (Table 4.2). Because the track placements in this school are permanent, the stable ability indicators are more appropriate for making these permanent placements than the unstable effort indicators are. Yet, although effort is less appropriate than ability for making permanent track placements, Tables 4.5 and 4.6 show that, in fact, the effort indicators have more influence than the ability indicators. Effort is more important than ability for the track placements of male and female students. Indeed, it is three times as important for female students. Similarly, Table 4.6 demonstrates that the unique influence of the effort indicators on track changes is not only greater than that of the ability indicators but is even greater than the total influence of the ability indicators (e.g.,unique plus shared variance). Therefore, even if all the shared variance could be attributed to ability (which is highly unlikely), effort would still have greater influence than ability. For both track placement and track change, effort indicators are at least as important, and usually much more important, than ability indicators. We may conclude that Grayton's permanent track placements tend to be more often based on unstable than on stable criteria.

Conclusions.   This chapter's data tell us that few, if any, selection criteria in this track system have appropriate properties (validity, stability) for justifying permanent placements, that none are appropriately applied (universalistically) to resemble a meritocracy, that a single criterion (IQ) is applied in different ways at different stages of the selection process, and that the criteria most heavily relied on for making track placements are the least appropriate for this track structure. These findings have several kinds of implications.

These findings are revealing of school values. Chapter 3 notes that the tournament system, like a contest system avoids conferring elite status until the very end and thereby discourages the formation of an aristocracy. This chapter shows that the tournament system also resembles a contest system in basing elite status on "the aspirant's own efforts" (Turner, 1960). Basing selections on effort also discourages aristocratic attitudes, for those granted elite status must continue to exert effort to maintain that status (except in the upper college track). They must be industrious and maintain their attendance. They cannot rely on their abilities or on the achievements they might accomplish effortlessly. By demanding effort from the chosen elite, the track system prevents the chosen students from slipping into an easy reliance on ability that might appear aristocratic. Like Turner's contest model, Grayton's tournament model based on effort discourages the formation of an aristocracy.

Yet the main problems with the Grayton selection criteria are not in the values they reflect but in their application and properties. Because no criterion is universalistically applied, placements seem somewhat arbitrary. Furthermore, the instability of effort indicators indicates that they reflect transitory behaviors, presumably dependent on evanescent motivational and situational circumstances. Arbitrary and transitory criteria may be appropriate for an open contest system in which "elite status . . . is taken by the aspirant's own efforts." But the tournament system is open only for allowing students to lose elite status by their lack of effort; it does not allow students to take elite status by their own efforts. No amount of effort (or ability) is sufficient for regaining elite status once it is lost. The result is permanent placement based on arbitrary and transitory criteria at a single point in time. Any temporary absence of effort leads to permanent loss of college-track status. Tracking solidifies one set of scores in an unwarranted manner.

Since real social systems rarely correspond exactly to their ideals, the failure of the meritocratic model may not seem surprising. Furthermore, Jencks and his associates (1972) have already shown that school criteria do not have much bearing on educational attainment. Yet our results are much more striking, for we discover that school criteria do not exert a decisive influence on placement in Grayton's own system. If society does not respond appropriately to criteria, this may indicate differential commitment to criteria by different segments of society. But if a single, highly controlled system does not respond appropriately to its own criteria, this must indicate the absence of a strong commitment to an appropriate selection policy.[11]

Is a meritocracy possible? This analysis suggests not. Grayton High School is a setting where meritocratic selection is particularly likely, if it ever were possible. Because Grayton High School has a socially homogeneous student body, social class and racial discrimination cannot interfere with the application of meritocratic selection. It is a single, highly controlled institution that systematically collects many evaluative indicators of merit. It implements a track system that channels opportunity, presumably for the sake of meritocratic efficiency. The failure of the Grayton track system to meet the requirements of the meritocratic model suggests that few schools are likely to implement meritocratic selection. Given the central role of school in executing meritocratic selection for society, we must infer that meritocracy is an unlikely form of selection.

Furthermore, there is good reason to suspect that meritocracy is not really desired. Despite the apparent attractions of meritocratic selection, school staff—the people who have to administer meritocratic selection—do not find it attractive. Their reports suggest that the very objectivity and detachment of IQ scores make these scores far less compelling than the staff's subjective evaluations, ratings, and grades (see Chapter 10). And the precision of universalistic selections similarly contradicts their personal preferences. These feelings of Grayton's school staff are likely to be widespread, and they are a further reason to suppose that a meritocratic policy based on objective criteria is not likely to be implemented.

Choosing appropriate selection criteria is a thorny problem for society, and "delegating the problem to the schools is a way of sweeping it under the rug" (Jencks et al., 1972, p. 136). Given the lack of a value consensus about criteria, the limitations of the available indicators of merit, and the problems of implementing universalistic objective selection, an explicit universalistic policy may be impossible and undesirable. The flexible and judicious balancing of criteria by a professional counselor may be the best way to make suitable placements. But the counselor's discretion does not allow him to impose his own fleeting impressions in place of teachers' global ratings, to select some students arbitrarily on IQ and others on effort—picking and choosing as he wishes, or to create permanent selections largely based on unstable criteria. If society cannot reach a consensus on a meritocratic policy (universalistically based on valid and stable criteria), then it must reject the meritocratic model, its presumed efficiencies, and its early permanent placements. Flexibility and discretion in criteria also require flexibility and discretion in the opportunity structure, and they suggest the need for eliminating early placements (see Chapter 10).

What then is the value of the meritocratic model? Why have political leaders and school administrators so persistently paraded this vision before our eyes only to allow its realization to be unfulfilled? Certainly, the meritocratic model does not help society or schools to make these selections, for it ignores the difficulties involved in reaching a consensus on a valid and stable criterion. But, like Plato's myth of men of different metals —which does not assist in the realization of meritocratic selections—the meritocratic model justifies unequal opportunity and privileges and distracts people's awareness from the failures of the actual selection system. Similarly, by concealing the criterion problem within school track systems, political leaders and school administrators can use the meritocratic model as a myth to delude us about the way educational selection actually operates and to justify illegitimate inequalities.

APPENDIX: MEANS, STANDARD DEVIATIONS, AND CODING FOR REGRESSION ANALYSES

IQ and attendance are continuous variables: IQ is the raw score on the Otis test, and attendance is the number of days a student

Variable	Mean		Standard Deviation	
	Boys	Girls	Boys	Girls
IQ	104.46	105.61	11.27	11.91
Teacher's ability rating	2.88	2.41	.81	.81
Industry	1.69	1.48	.35	.33
Attendance	9.49	9.36	7.73	8.24
Deportment	1.81	1.96	.31	.14
Track placement	1.69	1.52	.47	.50
Track change	1.35	1.22	.48	.42

missed during the school year (multiplied by minus one). Teacher's ability rating, industry, and deportment are each four-category ordinal scales from one to four. Track placement is one if college track, zero if noncollege track. Track change is one if shift out of college track, zero if stay in college track.

Notes

1. It seems that even schools that have difficulty executing their teaching function are able to continue their evaluative function, and, indeed, such schools seem to place even more emphasis on the completeness of their records.
2. All analyses in Chapters 4 and 5 use the sample of 192 students, described in the Appendix to Chapter 2, unless otherwise noted.
3. Because grades are conceptually related to both ability and effort (although empirically related only to the latter), I shall not include grades in the following analyses. This does not alter my results empirically, as footnote eight indicates.
4. I have not analyzed the predictive validity of these indicators because I lack independent measures of the attributes. Obviously, I cannot use college admissions as a measure of ability, for college admissions may be directly based on IQ scores themselves (rather than on the attribute that IQ purports to measure). Because I do not possess college grades, I cannot use them, although one might even suspect that they could be influenced by the labeling effects of IQ scores.
5. There are several possible reasons for the discrepancy between Bloom's correlations and Grayton's. One reason might be the difference in IQ tests: the studies that Bloom cites use the Stanford–Binet, and the Grayton school system uses the Otis. The Stanford–Binet had two main components, verbal

and performance, but the Otis tests only the verbal component. Since performance IQ requires the quick solution of puzzles with blocks and cards, manual dexterity is an important component of performance IQ, and it is not surprising that performance test scores stabilize by the age of 9 (by which time children's manual coordination is nearly fully developed). Verbal tests are based on vocabulary skills, which continue to develop, and verbal test scores continue to change throughout adolescence and early adulthood. Although the overall Stanford–Binet score, which includes early developed performance skills, is much more stable than the Otis, the verbal component of the Stanford–Binet is not much more stable than the Otis score.

A second reason for the discrepancy is the greater homogeneity of the IQ distribution of the Grayton sample ($s.d. = 11$) than of the IQ distributions in most of the samples in Bloom's studies ($s.d. = 15$). Because correlations are used as the measure of stability and shifts of rank order are more likely (and less important) in more homogeneous samples (where numbers are close together), we would expect less stability in Grayton's homogeneous sample.

The third reason for the divergence is far more interesting. Not only are the IQ scores in the Grayton sample more homogeneous, but also the environmental characteristics of Grayton are more homogeneous. Because the studies quoted by Bloom tend to have diverse social classes in their samples, and because these diverse social environments tend to remain constant and have a continuing influence on the IQ scores of the individuals in the sample, social class differences would have a stabilizing influence on the rank order of IQs in these environments, but this would not be true in Grayton, which had no such class differences.

Unfortunately, this study is not able to investigate these issues, for we lack comparable studies on the Otis test in heterogeneous settings. Although group-administered tests like the Otis are far more widely used than individually administered tests like the Standford–Binet, very little research on the stability or validity of the Otis has been done. Chapter 7 will explore some of the structural sources of instability of IQ in Grayton.

(Note that, although Bloom also reported correlations corrected for attenuation, the raw correlations in his studies were the ones reported here.)

6.   For testing the model, a single scale of positions is required. Since it is not certain that the six different track positions form a single scale,this analysis will collapse the six track positions into the single dichotomy that is the main distinction in track placement, the distinction between college and noncollege tracks. For all the analyses in the remainder of this chapter, track placement will refer to placement in a college track versus a noncollege track, and track change will refer to changes across this distinction.

Also, for the sake of simplicity, the SCAT scores are not included in these analyses. They are sufficiently highly correlated with IQ to be virtually the same indicator. Although they might have been combined into a single scale with IQ, that would obscure much of the analysis, particularly since all the other scales would be single indicators.

7.   The greater predictive power in the lower interval is more true for some indicators than for others. It is particularly true for grades and deportment, which predict track placement quite poorly at the top of their scales, but which predict nearly perfectly at the bottom of their scales. The analysis of the end intervals takes us beyond the simple summary statement of a statistical measure of association to a more detailed description of the relationship. The association of track placement and grade point average (GPA) is similar to the association of track placement and IQ,

teachers' rating, or industry (gamma statistics for each are respectively: GPA, 69; IQ, .73; teacher's rating, .66; industry, .77). Yet Table 4.3 shows that high GPA predicts track placement worse than high values of these other indicators, but low GPA predicts it much better than low values of these other indicators.

8. Deportment and grade point average are not included in the regressions. Deportment is not included, because it is so poorly associated with track placement and track change, never explaining even 1% of the unique variance in regressions. Grade point average is not included, because it does not fit the conceptual split between ability and effort and because it is so highly associated with industry. Grade point average would not explain more than 2% unique variance in these regressions: track placement (1% boys, 0% girls), track change (0% boys, 2% girls). Adding them into the analyses would not alter our findings.

The reader is reminded that social class variables are not included here, because social class does not really vary in this community (see Chapter 2). When fathers' education and occupation and mothers' education are included, they explain less than 2% total variance for both boys' and girls' track placement (1% boys, 2% girls).

9. The proper method of predicting membership in a class from continuous predictors is multiple discriminate analysis. However, in the specific case of a two-value dependent variable, multiple discriminate analysis is identical to multiple regression analysis of a 0–1 coded dummy variable upon the predictors (Tatsuoka, 1971).

10. The reader may conjecture that the greater number of levels on IQ and attendance than in teacher's ability rating and industry might give the former variables superior explanatory power. Yet, when IQ and attendance are grouped into four categories with similar distributions to teacher's ability rating and industry, the results are unchanged.

11. Chapter 2 notes that track placements are centrally control-
     led by a few administrators, and the virtually perfect corres-
     pondence between English and history track assignment
     suggests that universalistic placements are possible.

Chapter 5   Tracking: Society's Switchyard

The school feels that the curricula should meet the needs of all the students. It prepares for college those students who have the ability . . . to continue their education beyond the high school level. . . . The school realizes that many of its students do not have the scholastic aptitude to go on to college. For these students the school feels an obligation to provide programs and materials that will enable the students to make their lives productive (Grayton student handbook).

By definition, tracking selects and groups students on the basis of certain criteria and, having offered appropriate preparation, allocates them to the positions in society for which they are most suited. Thus the meritocratic analysis of tracking must extend beyond the selection and grouping processes within the microcosm of the school to an analysis of the way that tracking channels students into appropriate societal positions. As the quotation from the Grayton student handbook makes clear, meritocratic allocation to society is the cornerstone of the school's purpose. The track system is neither just an educational curriculum for enhancing student growth nor an organizational plan for promoting efficient school operation. Rather, it is a societal institution whose ultimate justification lies in its effectiveness for meritocratic allocation of students into societal positions.

Sociologists have traditionally been interested in the transition between school and society, but few have investigated the role of tracking in this process. Parsons discusses the ways that schools "allocate . . . human resources within the role structure of the adult society" (Parsons, 1959, p. 297), but his discussion is general and not based on systematic empirical analysis. Numerous other sociologists have shown interest in the relationship of tracking and societal allocation (e.g. Hollingshead, 1949; Sexton, 1961; Schafer and Olexa, 1971), but none has presented systematic longitudinal data on these issues. Some stratification research has begun to analyze longitudinal data on the relationship of schooling and societal allocation (Sewell and Shah, 1967; Sewell et al., 1970), yet that research has not investigated the role of tracking in this process.

Jencks and his colleagues (1972) have produced a systematic empirical analysis of the relationship of tracking to societal allocation. Using the Project Talent longitudinal data, they find that "about sixty percent of the ninth graders who were in college preparatory curriculums in 1960 entered college in 1964, compared to eighteen percent of those in other curriculums" (*ibid.*, p. 157). After IQ, grades, and social class are controlled for, the difference between college and noncollege curriculums is reduced to 44% and 32%, so that tracking accounts for about 12% of the variation in college attendance (*ibid.*, p. 158). The authors conclude their extensive analysis of the many possible school influences on educational attainment by stating that "the curriculum to which a student is assigned is the one measurable factor that influences attainment" (*ibid.*, p. 159).

Jencks and his colleagues do not investigate the relationship of tracking to job status and income. They do find that educational attainment, a correlate of tracking, has little influence on job status and income. We might infer that tracking, being a form of educational selection which precedes educational attainment, might also be unrelated to job outcomes.

Yet there are important shortcomings in Jencks's analyses. Jencks studies these issues for a large nationwide sample, and this approach forces him to rely on indicators of tracking which are of dubious validity. The analyses, which purport to investigate tracking, actually use students' descriptions of their tracks. As Jencks admits in a footnote, "students' descriptions of their curriculum may simply be another measure of whether they plan to attend college" (*ibid.*, p. 174, No. 71).

Jencks's survey approach also leads him to average the effects of all kinds of track systems in all kinds of communities as if all operate in the same way. This tends to becloud the relationships involved. Using a more detailed description of a single track system, Hollingshead (1949) finds that tracking (with social class) exerts an important influence on job placements (although he cannot control for social class). Using detailed case studies of work organizations, Berg (1971) observes that employers rely heavily on educational credentials as the basis of hiring and promotion.

In summary we see contradictory assertions and findings. The definition of tracking and the Grayton student handbook's description of tracking both assume that tracking affects students' placements in society. Jencks and his colleagues provide some support for this assumption, by noting that tracking influences college attendance, but they do not support the assumption of the influence on jobs. On the other hand, Hollingshead and Berg indicate that education may influence jobs.

The inadequacies of data and the conflicting observations of the available research point up the need for further probing of tracking's role in societal placements. By investigating these topics in a socially homogeneous school with a strong commitment to tracking, this study should be in a better position to clarify the relationships and processes. Furthermore, because this analysis extends the previous analyses of the opportunity structure and the criteria of tracking, this chapter can show the continuities between the operation of tracking within the school and its operation in the transition between school and society.

Of course, to be effective, tracking must do more than simply coordinate school curriculum and societal placement. Tracking's definition requires that it operate meritocratically in allocating students into society. If tracking is effective, then a student's ability and school performance will be important determinants of his later societal position, and tracking will be the mechanism through which this happens. There are, therefore, two fundamental questions for assessing tracking:

1. Are societal placements based on ability and school performance?
2. To what extent does tracking mediate this process?

These are the issues this chapter investigates.

Two basic differences appear in the placements of Grayton's graduates. One is the distinction between students who attend college and those who do not. The second is the distinction among jobs for those who do not attend college. Part I of this chapter investigates the factors influencing college attendance, and Part II investigates the factors influencing job placements.

PART I: SCHOOL INFLUENCES ON COLLEGE ATTENDANCE

The Dependent Variables.   The school guidance counselors survey all graduates of the high school in the fall following their graduation to find out what schools or occupations the students have chosen. Like all other records kept by Grayton, this survey is complete—it has a 100% response rate. Furthermore, the information seems reliable, for it corresponds well with information I gathered from a random sample of 50 of these students in follow-up interviews.[1]

Roughly one-fifth of the Grayton graduates attend four-year colleges. Among those who do not, most take full-time jobs, some enroll in vocational schools, and a few enroll in junior colleges. Because the admission requirements of the vocational schools are not very stringent, and because the jobs for which these schools offer preparation are not so different from the skilled jobs that many Grayton graduates obtain immediately after high school, these schools are grouped with the noncollege category for the analyses of Part I. Junior colleges are the most difficult to categorize, because students completing two years of junior college are not guaranteed admission to four-year colleges, and thus their opportunities are different from those of their peers in four-year colleges (see Clark, 1960). The inclusion of these students in either group would dilute the strength of relationships; since there are only 21 students in this group, most analyses in this chapter do not include them. The dependent variable of Part I is the distinction between those enrolled in four-year colleges and those in jobs or vocational schools.

This distinction is important. College attendance is a key determinant of a person's career. Admittedly, this is less true in this decade than in previous decades. As a greater proportion of youth began attending college, college attendance may have become less important as a sign of elite status, and the relative income advantages to college-educated workers over noncollege workers has declined (owing in part to the abundance of college-educated job seekers and the successes of blue-collar unions). But these recent changes have not eradicated the social and economic benefits of college attendance. Freeman (1975) has shown that the economic returns to college education have decreased somewhat from 1959 to 1974 (from 11% to 8.5%), but even the high tuitions of the 1970's lead to large financial returns on the investment. College graduates still earn considerably more than those who do not attend college.

College also leads to important social gains. In the first place, college attendance is itself a direct determinant of social status. People accord respect and prestige to people who have received a college education. Furthermore, college-educated applicants are given preference for white-collar jobs, and these jobs, even relatively low-paying ones, offer higher social status than blue-collar jobs. Indeed, a white collar, a desk, and the avoidance of back-breaking or manual work are symbols of status in our society. For the immediately foreseeable future, and for the greater part of the lives of the youths we are studying here, a college education will be an important social and economic advantage. It is important, therefore, to see how students' high school experiences determine whether or not they attend college.

The Relative Influences of School Factors on College Attendance.   To explore the relationship of students' ability and effort to college attendance, I performed regression analyses of college attendance on the various school record indicators: IQ, teacher's rating of ability, industry, deportment, and attendance (see Table 5.1).[2] For the most part these results are similar to the regression analyses of college-track placement in Chapter 4. Not surprisingly, student ability and effort are less good predictors of college attendance than of track placement, but the difference is surprisingly small; they have nearly as much influence on attendance at many diverse colleges as they do on track placement within the school.

Furthermore, their influence on college attendance shows generally the same pattern as on track placement. For girls, ability and effort have equal influence on college attendance, just as they do on track placement. For boys, effort has much more influence than ability on college attendance, just as it does on track placement.

These are strange findings. They indicate that college admissions committees at diverse schools, ranging from Harvard to the local state colleges, tend to value ability and effort to the same degree and in the same proportion as the high school does in making track placements. Of course, stated in this manner, this interpretation appears absurd. There must be some intervening

TABLE 5.1. REGRESSION ANALYSIS OF COLLEGE ATTENDANCE ON ABILITY AND EFFORT*

	Boys		Girls	
Criteria	Unique Variance (%)	Total Variance (%)	Unique Variance (%)	Total Variance (%)
Ability	11	20	10	11
Effort	16	25	13	14
Shared	10		1	
Total	36		24	

*Ability is composed of variance explained by IQ and teachers' recommendations. Effort is composed of variance explained by industry, deportment, and attendance.

factor to produce this symmetry; the most likely candidate would be tracking itself.

Table 5.2 shows the regression of college attendance on ability, effort, and twelfth grade track placement. For both boys and girls, track placement alone explains college attendance far better than all the ability and effort indicators combined (either total or unique variances being compared). For girls, track placement

TABLE 5.2. REGRESSION ANALYSIS OF COLLEGE ATTENDANCE ON ABILITY, EFFORT, AND TWELFTH GRADE TRACK PLACEMENT*

	Boys		Girls	
Criteria	Unique Variance (%)	Total Variance (%)	Unique Variance (%)	Total Variance (%)
Ability	1	20	2	11
Effort	7	25	2	14
Track	16	44	34	55
Shared	28		20	
Total	52		58	

*Ability is composed of variance explained by IQ and teachers' recommendations. Effort is composed of variance explained by industry, deportment, and attendance.

explains virtually all the variation of college attendance that is explained; no single indicator explains even 1% of the remaining variance. Similarly, after a boy is placed in the college track in senior year, his ability does not have any bearing on his college attendance, although his effort has a modest influence (beyond its relationship to track placement). Because most of the influence of ability and effort on college attendance is shared with track placement, we may infer that track placement serves as a mediating mechanism that selects students by using the same criteria that colleges use for selection.

These findings are consistent with the assumptions underlying Grayton's tournament structure. The early permanent placement of students into noncollege tracks can be justified only if this placement is based on the same criteria that colleges use for admissions. Although tracking is not totally derived from ability and effort indicators, tracking seems to reflect these indicators to the same degree and in the same proportion as colleges use them for admissions. Furthermore, tracking does not seem to miss any students that colleges want to admit. The early track placements seem, therefore, to select students effectively on the same criteria as colleges require.

But this is only part of the story. Table 5.2 shows that, to a large extent, college attendance is explained by track placement uniquely, independent of all the ability and effort indicators. After ability and effort indicators have explained as much college attendance as they can (including influence they share with track placement), track placement uniquely explains half again this amount for boys (16%) and an additional one and one-half times this amount for girls (34%). Thus, the track placement label takes on a life of its own, even when it signifies nothing about ability and effort. This finding will be explored in the following sections.

Regression analysis is useful in determining the relative influence of several variables but not in revealing the absolute degree of association between variables. The preceding analyses account for about half of college attendance variance but like the glass of water perceived by the optimist and the pessimist, an explanatory power of 50% may be interpreted as a little or a lot, depending on one's inclinations. The problems of regression analyses are compounded because 100% explanation in a regression is often impossible. Some of the criticism of Jencks's interpretations focuses on the irreconcilable issue of how much is a lot.

If we want to see how track placement determines college attendance, simple tables will provide more appropriate descriptions of the degree of association. Table 5.3, portraying this relationship for boys and girls, is comparable to the preceding regressions (the junior college group omitted). It reveals several facts not suggested by the regression analysis.

In the first place, it points out that the relationship is nearly perfect. According to the regressions, about half of the variance of college attendance is explained by track position, and hence, much of college attendance is unexplained. Yet, the table tells us that the college attendance (and nonattendance) of only 7 boys and 9 girls out of a total of 171 students are unexplained by track placement. Although around 50% of the *variance* of college attendance is explained by track position, more than 90% of the individual *placements* are explained.

The table also reveals a pattern to the exceptions. There are many more college-track students excluded from college attendance that there are noncollege-track students included in college attendance. Actually, this relationship is even more dramatic when the individual exceptions are inspected. All but one of the

TABLE 5.3.   COLLEGE ATTENDANCE BY TRACKS FOR BOYS AND GIRLS

College Attendance	Boys		Girls	
	College Track (%)	Noncollege Track (%)	College Track (%)	Noncollege Track (%)
No college	14.8	95.5	20.0	95.2
Four-year college	85.2	4.5	80.0	4.8
Total	100.0	100.0	100.0	100.0
Number of cases	(27)	(67)	(35)	(42)

noncollege-track students who attend a four-year college had to go out of state (and quite far away) to find a college that would admit them. Furthermore, these students are the only Grayton graduates to attend college out of state. Noncollege-track students have virtually no possibility of attending college within the state system. The opportunity for college attendance after school is just like that for college-track placement within the school. The tournament system continues to apply: college attendance, like college-track placement, is possible but not ensured for those in college tracks and virtually impossible for those in noncollege tracks.

The Upper College Track and College Attendance.   We have seen that the distinction between college and noncollege tracks channels students into or away from attending colleges. But what is the function of the distinction between the upper and the lower college tracks? Table 5.4 displays the relationship of these tracks to college attendance. Two main distinctions stand out. First, 70% of the boys in upper college track attend prestige colleges, but only 5% of those in lower college track do so.[3] Second, although college-track position does not ensure college attendance,

TABLE 5.4.   COLLEGE ATTENDANCE BY COLLEGE TRACKS FOR BOYS AND GIRLS

	Boys		Girls	
College Attendance	Upper College Track (%)	Lower College Track (%)	Upper College Track (%)	Lower College Track (%)
No college	10.0	15.8	25.0	16.2
Junior college	0.0	15.8	0.0	16.2
Four-year college	20.0	62.8	50.0	62.2
Prestige four-year college	70.0	5.6	25.0	5.4
Total	100.0	100.0	100.0	100.0
Number of cases	(10)	(19)	(4)	(37)

upper-college-track position does virtually guarantee that students will attend college. Only one boy and one girl in the upper college track did not attend a four-year college.[4] In Chapter 3 it was noted that the upper college track operates like Turner's sponsored norm in ensuring continued stability of status over the entire school career. These findings indicate that the students in upper college track continue to be sponsored after graduation, guaranteed of college attendance, and given sole access to—and a high probability of—attendance at a prestige college.

The Perpetuation of Tracking in College Admissions.   A marked resemblance between Grayton's track placements and college attendance has twice been noted. First, it was noted that both use the same criteria. Now, we have seen that the opportunity structure within the track system resembles the opportunity structure from track placement to college admissions. Why is there such a close association between the track system and college admissions?

There are several possible explanations. Conceivably, the Grayton school administrators have chosen to use the same criteria for track placements that they know college admissions committees use. But this does not explain why track placement has such a large influence independent of any indicators of ability or effort.

Another possibilty is that the college track, particularly the upper college track, provides the sort of training that colleges feel is required for success in college. If this were the case, then colleges might purposely choose students from the college tracks and give them preference because of their superior training. Obviously, this must be true to some extent, because a student with inadequate preparation would be a poor risk for college admission. Yet the course requirements for college track are far in excess of what most colleges require. In fact, many general-track students take all the courses required by college admission standards. Yet virtually none of these students, not even those high in ability, grade point average, industry, and attendance, are admitted to colleges within the state. It is hard to believe that *all* colleges in this state place more weight on a student's track placement than on a student's ability and performance. Can it be that so many colleges hold such credence in the track system in this school?

Having doubted the two previous possibilities, we must consider the possibility that colleges favor the upper tracks unquestioningly and perhaps unwittingly. From interviews with the school administrators, I discovered that the school constructs a list of student class ranks that college admissions committees consider important. Some colleges consider applicants only in the top third of their class; others consider class rank as one of many criteria for admissions. It is important, therefore, to see what goes into such a scale.

Administrators claim that class rank mostly corresponds to achievement, being based on the rank order of grade point averages. But they cautioned that it is not fair to compare the grades of students in different tracks, for it is more difficult to get a particular grade in a higher track than in a lower one. Fairness demands that grades be weighted according to the track a student is in. Only upper-college-track students get full weighting for their grades. Lower-college-track students receive only three-quarters weighting, upper-business and upper-general-track students receive one-half weighting, and lower-business and lower-general-track students receive one-quarter weighting. On a four-point grade scale, this weighting formula effectively penalizes each successively lower level by one letter grade. Students in the lower general track would have to get an A average to have the same class rank as students in the upper college track with a D average! Thus, in using this weighting formula for computing class ranks, the school leads college admissions committees to rely unwittingly on track placement in their decisions.

The administrators' justification of the weighting formula seems plausible, and weighting grades by track is a common practice. Yet it is based on an assumption deserving attention. The justification of grade weighting assumes that grades are based on a student's rank within his track, and, consequently, that a certain grade in an upper track is harder to get than that same grade in a lower track. When, however, we look at the actual grades given in each track, we see that grades do not correspond to a student's rank within a track (see Table 5.5). The B average student is in the bottom third of the upper college track and in the top 20% of the lower general track. Clearly, grades do not indicate a student's rank in his track.

Although the administrators' contention seems reasonable, the facts are just the contrary. More than 90% of all As are given to the two college tracks. In fact, the proportion of As and Bs is directly related to the track. Instead of the grade-weighting formula's compensating for a grading bias against higher-track students, it supplements and extends an already existing grading distribution that penalizes *lower-track* students.

The results of adding favoritism to privilege are further illustrated by a version of Table 5.5 that reflects the weighting of each track. Table 5.6 presents the number of individuals in each track who receive a given ranking (which equals grades multiplied by track weighting). Obviously, all the top-ranking students are in

TABLE 5.5.   GRADE POINT AVERAGE BY TRACK PLACEMENT (GROUPED BY WEIGHTING)

| | Track | | | |
Grade Point Average	Upper College (%)	Lower College (%)	Upper Noncollege (%)	Lower Noncollege (%)
GPA = A	64.3	17.5	3.0	1.1
GPA = B	21.4	45.6	51.5	20.5
GPA = C	14.3	31.6	39.4	51.1
GPA = D	0.0	5.3	3.0	26.1
Total	100.0	100.0	100.0	100.0
Number of cases	(14)	(57)	(32)	(87)

χ^2 = 84.2 with 12 df

Gamma = 0.62

TABLE 5.6.   CLASS RANK BY TRACK PLACEMENT (GROUPED BY
WEIGHTING)

Class Rank	(Class Percentile)	Track			
		Upper College	Lower College	Upper Noncollege	Lower Noncollege
1	(95%+)	9			
2	(88%+)	3	10		
3	(73%+)	2	26	1	
4	(54%+)	0	18	17	1
5	(36%+)		3	13	18
6	(12%+)			1	45
7	(0%+)				23
Total		14	57	32	87

the upper college track, and all students in the top two ranks are
in the two college tracks. Furthermore, because of the distribution of grades in each track, all but one of the students in the top
three ranks are in the college tracks. In other words, all but 1 of
the top 50 students (e.g., the top quartile of the class) are in
college tracks. Whereas fewer than 1% of noncollege-track students are in the top quartile, all the upper-college-track students
and more than 60% of the lower-college-track students are in this
range. The double "compensation" of grade distribution and the
weighting formula clearly delineates the different tracks in the
class ranking. In so doing, the class rank formula effectively
prevents students in the noncollege tracks from being considered
for college admissions while effectively sponsoring students in
the upper-college track with a guarantee of college attendance
and preference for prestige college positions.

The previous chapter concluded that the Grayton track system
is largely a tournament system partially based on inappropriate
criteria and partially based on what seems to be unsystematic
application of criteria. This chapter spells out the implications of
this system for college admissions. Because grade weighting effectively transmits Grayton's track placements to the many college admissions committees throughout the state, these committees
unwittingly become a victim of the school track system, continu-

ing to promote the school's early selections based on inappropriate criteria or on unsystematic placements.

The preceding analyses have ignored distinctions among noncollege tracks and job placements. Yet Young's conception of meritocracy has its most intriguing and far-reaching implications when applied to the work world, for it is here that meritocracy leads to increased productivity and efficiency for society. Indeed, the origin of vocational tracks was premised on the efficiency of matching vocational training and job placements with ability and school performance (Callahan, 1962).

The Noncollege Tracks.   There are two kinds of distinctions among the noncollege tracks. The distinction between the business and general tracks represents a curriculum distinction. The business track offers a vocational curriculum in business skills (e.g., filing, bookkeeping, typing, and business mathematics) but does not permit students to take academic subjects (like foreign language, science, or algebra). The general track offers most kinds of academic courses (although at a less demanding level than their college-track equivalents) but does not allow students to enroll in most vocational (business) courses. Students choose whether they will be in the business or general tracks, this choice determining whether they will be in a highly regimented vocational curriculum or in a general nonvocational curriculum.

In contrast, the distinction between the upper and lower levels within the business or general tracks is not a matter of choice; the school counselors make that decision. The upper business and upper general tracks are meant to offer better preparation for those students who can profit from it. Guidance counselors state that they select the "better" noncollege-track students for these tracks.

As noted previously, tracking has two main purposes: to group students according to appropriate characteristics and to provide different groups with the most suitable preparation for their later life. The distinction between college and noncollege tracks attempts to perform both functions simultaneously. In contrast, the distinctions among noncollege tracks appear to separate these functions: the upper/lower-track distinction represents grouping by individual characteristics ("better" vs. "worse" students), and the business/general-track distinction represents the different job preparations offered to students (vocational vs. general). The rest of this section probes the selection criteria for these two track distinctions, and the following section explores the relationship of these distinctions to students' job placements.

The track definitions imply that ability and school performance should be more highly associated with the upper/lower-track distinction (the upper business and general tracks vs. the lower business and general tracks) than with the business/general-track distinction (the upper and lower business tracks vs. the upper and lower general tracks). But regression analyses of the school record indicators on these two track variables provide little support for this expectation (Table 5.7). The school record indicators are no more related to the upper/lower-track distinction than they are to the distinction between business and general tracks.

There are important sex differences in these regressions. The school record indicators explain less than 9% of the noncollege-track placements of the male students but more than 20% of the noncollege-track placements of female students. These are the first regressions where these indicators explain more track placement variance for females than for males.

These are also the first to display placements based more on ability than on industry, grades, and attendance. Whereas male and female college-track placements, track changes, and college attendance tend to be more influenced by effort than by ability, the female noncollege-track placements are based more on meritocratic criteria than on unstable indicators of transitory behaviors.

These distinctive data suggest that the Grayton track system is

TABLE 5.7. REGRESSION ANALYSIS OF NONCOLLEGE TRACKS ON
ABILITY AND EFFORT*

Criteria	Boys		Girls	
	Unique Variance (%)	Total Variance (%)	Unique Variance (%)	Total Variance (%)
Business vs. general tracks				
Ability	2	4	13	20
Effort	5	7	4	11
Shared	2		7	
Total	9		24	
Upper vs. lower tracks				
Ability	2	2	11	15
Effort	5	5	6	10
Shared	0		4	
Total	7		21	

*Ability is composed of variance explained by IQ and teacher's recommendations. Effort is composed of variance explained by industry, deportment, and attendance.

particularly concerned with the noncollege-track placements of female students. Their placements are more related to school record indicators and more related to meritocratic than nonmeritocratic indicators. Noncollege-track placements are particularly responsive to female students' attributes.

Job Placements. There are many ways to categorize the jobs taken by Grayton's graduates, but the distinction between skilled and unskilled is probably the most important. In the first place, this is a status distinction that is quite salient. When asked to group and rank a list of occupations according to social status, people consistently distinguish between skilled and unskilled jobs (Kahl, 1953, p. 77). When asked about their criteria for ranking social status, people tend to attribute their ranking to differences in skill and specialization (*ibid.*, p. 79). In the second place, this classification is relevant to our analysis of school effects, and it is more likely to correspond to ability, school performance, and training than other categorizations, such as prestige and income, would.

Because the noncollege tracks possess too few students (66 males and 45 females), and thus too few degrees of freedom, for analyzing all available variables, this section initially analyzes correlation coefficients to determine which variables have important influences. This paves the way for subsequent regression analyses of just the most important variables.

Table 5.8 presents the correlation coefficients of the job variable (skilled vs. unskilled job) with each of the school record indicators and the two track variables. These correlations indicate the following:

1. Most correlations for girls are considerably larger than those for boys.[5]
2. For girls, the two track variables, teacher's ability rating, industry, and deportment have significant correlations with job status.
3. For boys, the two track variables, IQ, and teacher's ability rating have significant, but small, correlations with job status.

Regression analyses of these variables (Table 5.9) show that nothing is particularly important for explaining the job status of male students, although effort and track variables explain female students' job status quite well. Industry, attendance, and deportment together do not explain even 1% of total variance of the male students' job status. The two ability indicators and the two track variables each uniquely explain only 6% , and they share 2%. In contrast, the effort variables explain a considerable amount of the girls' job status (19% uniquely) and ability and track variables each uniquely explain only 6%, and they share male students' track placements, those of the female students operate as intended, mediating some of the influence of the ability and effort variables (shared variance = 17%).

Again we see that the noncollege tracks are more responsive to females' school performance than to males'. The preceding sec-

TABLE 5.8. CORRELATIONS OF JOB STATUS WITH SCHOOL RECORD INDICATORS AND NONCOLLEGE TRACK VARIABLES FOR BOYS AND GIRLS

	IQ	Recommendation	Industry	Attendance	Deportment	Business/ General	Upper/ Lower
Boys	.21	.25	.02	.03	.09	.20	.25
Girls	.08	.37	.54	.18	.27	.28	.38

TABLE 5.9.   REGRESSION ANALYSIS OF JOB STATUS ON ABILITY,
EFFORT, AND NONCOLLEGE TRACK

	Boys		Girls	
Criteria	Unique Variance (%)	Total Variance (%)	Unique Variance (%)	Total Variance (%)
Ability	6	7	0	14
Effort	0	0	19	32
Track*	6	8	6	20
Shared	2		17	
Total	14		42	

*Track is composed of variance explained by the business/general distinction and the upper/lower distinction.

tion showed that both noncollege-track variables are more highly related to ability and school performance for females than for males. This section discovers the same to be true for job status. Noncollege-track male students cannot influence either their track placements or their job placements by their ability or effort. Noncollege-track female students, on the other hand, can modify their track placements by demonstrating high ability and can shape their ultimate job placements by exerting more effort, for both the noncollege tracks and the job world (immediately after high school) are more responsive to the school performance of female students.

The Actual Jobs.   The above analysis shows that the combination of industry, grades, and track position explains more than 40% of the variance of female students' job placement. We might conclude that school plays an important part in the kinds of jobs female graduates take.

Yet when we look at the specific jobs taken by these graduates, we see that these significant correlations are rather inconsequential. Among the 147 female graduates who took full-time jobs after graduation, a few are factory workers and a couple are para-professional workers (e.g., dental assistants), but more than

90% of the jobs are fairly similar: secretary, typist, teletype typist, key punch operator, clerk–typist, clerk, office girl, telephone operator, receptionist, sales clerk. For the preceding analysis, these jobs could be divided into those requiring the skill of typing and those not requiring it. Typing is a definite skill, and this is a real status distinction in an office staff. Yet, when we realize that typing can be acquired by one year of part-time study and that this distinction covers virtually the entire range of statuses that female graduates of the noncollege tracks can expect, then we cannot feel that the abilities, efforts, or track placements of these students have had much bearing on their careers.

In contrast, the distinction between skilled and unskilled jobs for males is more consequential. The skilled jobs that the males hold (medical technician, electrician, mechanic, telephone repairman, surveyor) clearly display more skill and probably confer greater status than the unskilled jobs (busboy, warehouseman, delivery boy, sales clerk, mail clerk, stock boy). Furthermore, these skilled jobs are likely to offer better pay and better career opportunities than the unskilled jobs.

Thus, although female students' abilities and efforts are reflected in their noncollege-track placements and their job placements, the distinctions among their jobs are rather inconsequential. Only the jobs offered to males seem to reflect important differences in status, and their jobs bear little or no relation to their abilities, efforts, or track placements.

Sex Differences in Tracking.   Schools are often accused of sexism (see Stacey et al., 1974). Furthermore, research indicates that schools are more likely to discriminate against working-class than against middle-class female students (see Alexander and Eckland, 1974). Therefore, it is not surprising to learn that this working-class school makes it harder for females than for males to be in college tracks. We see proportionately fewer females than males in college tracks (23% of females vs. 36% of males), and the female college-track placements are less related to ability and effort indicators than the male placements are (because proportionately more high-ability and high-effort females are in noncollege tracks).

Yet our analyses show just the opposite findings for noncollege tracks and for job placements. Although college-track placements (and college attendance) are not as responsive to female ability and effort, noncollege-track placements (and jobs) are more responsive to the ability and effort of females than of males. The business track, particularly the upper business track, is highly responsive to female ability and effort.

These findings are consistent with the administrators' obvious pride in the vocational program offered to business-track females. Although most of Grayton's vocational equipment is old and in poor condition, the typewriters are new and well maintained. The administrators say that the female business-track program is particularly demanding and rigorous. The principal seems proud when he states that "the business track doesn't allow students to waste their time with a lot of course electives. . . . [Business track females] must settle down and commit themselves to a tough curriculum." Perhaps because of these features, the business track is well respected in the community, and the administrators boast of the success they have at placing female business-track graduates in jobs. In contrast, the administrators do not volunteer much information about the business-track offerings for male students. These seem to be mostly simple clerical courses of which even the administrators do not speak highly.

The preceding data and the administrators' statements suggest that the noncollege tracks offer better training and more appropriate track and job placements for female than for male students. This finding indicates the double standard of the track system. If college-track males demonstrate high ability and effort, they are likely to remain in college tracks and ultimately to attend college; but this is much less true for females. If females demonstrate high ability and effort, the track system is responsive to them only after they have left the college tracks. Indeed, the business track's responsiveness to females constitutes an incentive for them to enter these tracks and receive preparation for inconsequential selections to dead-end jobs.

Conclusions.   This analysis began with two questions:

1. Are societal placements based on ability and school performance?
2. To what extent does tracking mediate this process?

College attendance and job placements were separately analyzed. The results can be summarized as follows:

College Attendance

1. College attendance is not completely explained by school criteria and is more affected by effort than by ability.
2. A student's ability and effort (during twelfth grade) have no bearing on college attendance after he has been placed in his twelfth grade track.
3. On the other hand, track position has a large unique influence on college attendance, even when it signifies nothing about a student's ability or effort.
4. Similar findings appear to be true for the influence of upper college track on college and prestige college attendance.

Job Placement

1. Ability and effort determine the noncollege-track placements of females more than of males. Similarly, ability, effort, and noncollege-track placements affect the job placements of females more than of males.
2. Yet there is very little difference among the jobs obtained by female graduates.

The contradictions in these results are tragic. During the six years of tracking, students are twice tested on ability and achievement, and they are rated on achievement, industry, attendance, and deportment six times each year on report cards (and virtually every day in their classes). Yet all of this has only a modest bearing on college attendance. College admissions decisions respond to these evaluations only insofar as they are reflected in track placement. Since tracking is only partially related to school evaluations and is more related to transitory than to stable criteria, college attendance perpetuates the same arbitrary selections as tracking.

Furthermore, these evaluations and track placements have virtually no effect on job placements. Where the job world appears to be responsive to female students' school performance and track placements, it is only to make a small status distinction of little consequence. Where the job world offers status distinctions to male high school graduates, the higher-status jobs are virtually unrelated to school variables. Although the job world may respond to gross categories of dropout and high school graduate, employers seem to show no interest in the many other evaluative categories and training program distinctions generated by the school.

The studies of Jencks and his colleagues (1972) suggest that these conclusions may be widespread. As seen earlier, Jencks notes that tracking exerts an important influence on college attendance and that school factors exercise little sway on job status. His analyses of nationwide survey data illustrate the same kind of relationships found in Grayton.

Yet, because of the difficulty in ensuring valid data and the risk of washing out effects through averaging unlike cases, Jencks's analyses are likely to understate the actual effects of tracking. Consequently, whereas Jencks finds that tracking has a probabilistic relation to college attendance, we observe that tracking can be categorically related to college attendance.[6] Similarly, we might infer that Jencks underestimates the sway that school factors exercise on job status, particularly because he did not look at the effects of vocational training programs. Yet my study, which does consider vocational tracking, replicates his finding. Even a single school, which creates elaborate track distinctions and extensive student evaluations for six years, has very little effect on the job placements of its graduates.

Chapter 3 showed that the Grayton track system operates like a tournament by creating continual selection, by allowing mobility in only one direction, and by removing those eliminated from any further selections. This chapter's observations make it clear that these aspects of the internal structure of tracking are maintained in the transition from graduation to colleges or jobs, a transition that is merely one more stage in the tournament. Noncollege-track students are prevented from attending four-year colleges and assured of attending junior colleges (if they wish); therefore, they do not experience any further educational selection. Although they experience job selections, most job placements are unrelated to students' abilities, efforts, or track placements, thus implying little selectivity in the allocation process. In addition, the general similarity of the placements and their limited opportunities for advancement further undermine selectivity. Tournament selection within the school also determines students' fates after school. Those eliminated from the school's tournament are also eliminated from the educational and occupational tournament as they enter society. High school tracking is quite literally a switchyard for society.

NOTES

1. Obviously, the students might have distorted both their responses to the school's questionnaire and to my questions, but I have no reason to suspect that they did.

2. As in Chapter 4, grade point average is not included in this chapter's regressions, because it does not fit the conceptual split between ability and effort and because it is so highly correlated with industry. If it were added to the regressions in this chapter, it would not alter the findings discussed here,

never explaining more than 2% unique variance for either college attendance (2% boys, 0% girls) or job status (0% boys, 1% girls).

3. The prestige of colleges was determined by asking three counselors which of the colleges that these students attended they would consider "prestige colleges." They showed almost perfect agreement on their selections. I would expect most people to agree with their judgments, except possibly for their inclusion of several good private colleges in the prestige category. What is prestigious for a working-class community may not be prestigious for a middle-class community. In part, this reflects the fact that working-class students can attend a large private university only if they are good enough to be awarded a scholarship, but middle-class students may be able to pay their own tuition.

4. The junior college group is included in this analysis. None of the upper-college-track boys or girls attend junior colleges, but more than 15% of the lower college-track boys and girls do so.

5. The standard deviation of girls' job status (.5056) is virtually identical to that of boys (.5061).

6. Furthermore, in his concern to find school factors with large unique influences, Jencks overlooks the fact that tracking is not supposed to have a unique influence—it is supposed to influence students' careers jointly with IQ and grades.

Chapter 6　　　　The Illusion of Choosing Fate

I n the two preceding chapters, the track system has been held up to the meritocratic model, and we have seen that it fails by most standards. No combination of school record indicators could be found that completely explains the track placements, track changes, or college or job placements. Perhaps, though, the wrong standards have been used. Could it be that track placements are based on students' choices?

Surely, the issue of choice is intrinsic to the stated purpose of offering different curricula. Furthermore, nearly all the Grayton noncollege-track students interviewed (26 of 30) stated that they chose the track they were in. Jencks presents a similar finding: "84 percent of all high school seniors [in the Coleman survey] said they were in the curriculum they wanted to be in" (Jencks et al.,

1972, p. 34). One might readily conclude that it is really students' own choices that determine track placements.

But the issue is not yet resolved. Why would students choose to enroll in a curriculum offering low status and low opportunities? Jencks suggests that students have several kinds of reasons.

> Some will choose curriculums that lead nowhere, because such curriculums involve less work in the short run. Some will eschew college, because they dislike the idea of spending 4 more years reading books. Some will avoid the high-status jobs, because they are afraid of responsibility or even of success. The fact that this happens does not prove that the student's educational opportunities were unequal; it proves that equal opportunity is not enough to ensure equal results (*ibid.,* p. 37).

Of course I must agree with Jencks that laziness, aversion to books, and fear of success do exist. But neither he nor we know why they exist or how they are related to tracking and aspirations. Are they early formed personality traits that are permanent determinants of choices or are they patterns of habits, beliefs, and values that are transitory responses to situations in our lives? The real question is whether laziness, aversion to books, and fear of success are the *causes* of lower-track placement or whether they are its *results*. The explanations that Jencks proposes themselves require explanations.

Do students in this school actually choose their track placements? How do students make track and career choices? How do they gather the information required for these choices? These questions are crucial for an understanding of social mobility. The massive literature on adolescent aspirations manifests the importance of these questions, and yet there is no research that investigates the process of making choices. The omission is understandable, for the actual choice process is hard to study. In the following sections, I will try to probe this process by drawing upon students' recollections and perceptions, by noting some of the obvious features of the guidance system, and by describing some actual interactions between students, parents, and guidance counselors. There are difficulties and limitations in each of these methods, and the information gleaned is incomplete, but the composite portrayal is highly suggestive. These findings not only produce an analysis of tracking choices, but they also raise profound questions about the possibilities of free and informed choice in any social institution.

Student Recollections. An obvious aspect of the choice process is the sequence of choices. Chapter 3 showed a clear pattern to the sequence of students' track choices in Grayton. The college track (called the language curriculum in seventh grade) was the initial track choice for most students in our sample. Of the seniors interviewed, the college track was the seventh grade choice for all the college-track sample, many of the business-track sample, and most of the general-track sample (see Chapter 3, Table 3.5). No one chose the college track as a second or third choice. The business track was the original choice for most of the business-track sample, and it was the second choice for the remainder. In contrast, the general track was the original choice for only two of those in the general-track sample, the second choice for many (12), and even the third choice for some (6).[1] Students' choices suggest that college track is most desired and general track is least desired, and yet students never choose to switch into a more desired track but only into a less desired track. If choice exists in this track system, it would seem to be free only in one direction.

When asked why they changed tracks, students offered two kinds of reasons: a preference for a different kind of curriculum or the necessity for an easier curriculum. Students who switched to business track offered these two reasons equally often. But students who switched to general track overwhelmingly (13 of 16) attributed their change to having failed or done poorly in another track. Therefore, the choice of general track is not only a second or third choice; it is also perceived as a choice derived more from necessity than from preference.

Choices, even second choices, may indicate commitment, for these students have chosen to continue coming to school. Therefore, the reasons that students offer to explain their commitment to their track can also elucidate the choice process. Students were asked why they chose the track they were in. The responses are shown in Table 6.1. Virtually all college-track students said that they were in their track to receive preparation for college. Virtually all the business-track students—even those who had originally chosen college track—said they were in their track to receive preparation for a job. In contrast, most general-track students said they were in their track "just for the diploma," and they could not think of any other reason to be there. This may indicate a choice, but the choice manifests no intrinsic interest in school itself.

When we speak of free choice of school curriculum, we assume that students can choose any curriculum—both "high" and "low," that they will get their first choice, and that their choice will have some meaning for them. The track choices in this school are not free by these standards.

Furthermore, the Grayton track system does not even allow a student's initial track selection to be a real choice. As noted in Chapter 3, the official policy stipulates that an individual can choose his track, but he cannot choose his level placement within a track, for level is determined by guidance counselors. Students have no say about the level in which they are placed, and yet that level has important implications for their future track placements. Students' reports of their seventh grade *level* placements within the language curriculum are highly related to their twelfth

TABLE 6.1.   REASON FOR TRACK CHOICE BY TRACK

Reason for Track Choice	Track		
	College Track	Business Track	General Track
Preparation for college	19	0	2
Job preparation	0	9	4
Just for the diploma	0	1	13
Other	1	0	1
	20	10	20

grade *track* placements (see Chapter 3, Table 3.5). Whereas more than three-quarters of the students in the top two levels are still in college track in twelfth grade, fewer than one-quarter of students in the lower levels remain in college track. Consequently, even the initial choice of college track is subverted by the system of levels.

Informed Choice.   To be meaningful, choice must be based on adequate information. The single most important kind of information needed to make an informed track choice is knowledge about what sort of preparation is offered by one's chosen track. In the questionnaire administered to a sample of one-third of the Grayton senior class, students were asked "How far do you *expect* you will actually go in school?" A student's educational expectation is not just a sign of future hope; it is also an indication of what preparation a student believes he has chosen, that is, what information he has about his chosen track.[2]

When students' educational expectations are compared with their track placements (see Table 6.2), rather clear patterns emerge. Virtually all students in the college tracks and the upper general track expect to attend college. The student expectations in the lower business and lower general tracks are more mixed, but the majority of students in these tracks expect to attend college, and so we may infer that college is seen as a reasonable option in these tracks. Only in the upper business track do a majority of students expect not to attend college. Thus, a majority of students in five of the six tracks believe they are receiving preparation that will permit them to go to college.

We already know that the facts are quite different from these expectations (see Chapter 5). Very few noncollege-track students actually attend colleges. Table 6.3 presents the actual pattern of college attendance of these same students in the year following their graduation. Virtually all college-track students expected to attend college, and nearly all did. Most upper-business-track students did not expect to attend college, and in fact they did not. But a large majority of students in the other three noncollege tracks did expect to attend college, and their expectations were

TABLE 6.2. EDUCATIONAL EXPECTATIONS BY TRACK

			Track (Senior Year)			
Educational Expectations	Upper College (%)	Lower College (%)	Upper Business (%)	Lower Business (%)	Upper General (%)	Lower General (%)
Expect college	100.0	94.7	28.6	59.1	100.0	67.4
Not expect college	0.0	5.3	71.4	40.9	0.0	32.6
Total	100.0	100.0	100.0	100.0	100.0	100.0
Number of cases	(14)	(57)	(21)	(44)	(12)	(43)

TABLE 6.3.   ACTUAL COLLEGE ATTENDANCE BY TRACK AND EXPECTATIONS*

	Track (Senior Year)					
	Upper College (%)	Lower College (%)	Upper Business (%)	Lower Business (%)	Upper General (%)	Lower General (%)
Expect college						
Attend college	85.7	84.1	9.6	11.3	16.6	16.2
Not attend college	14.3	10.6	19.0	57.8	83.4	51.2
Not expect college						
Attend college	0.0	0.0	0.0	0.0	0.0	0.0
Not attend college	0.0	5.3	71.4	40.9	0.0	32.6
Total	100.0	100.0	100.0	100.0	100.0	100.0
Number of cases	(14)	(57)	(21)	(44)	(12)	(43)

*"College" refers to junior college and four-year college.

113

largely disappointed. The contrast for the upper general track is so marked as to be pathetic: all these students expected to attend college, and yet only two were in college in the following year.

This table reveals a disturbing pattern of disappointment. But even more distressing is that students' choices exhibit a widespread misconception about the opportunities provided by the noncollege tracks. Students' track placements may reflect their choices, but their choices are not based on accurate information about tracking. Of course, when we realize that twelfth grade expectation reflects choice already tempered by six years of experience in tracking, it is all the more striking that, even in the last term of high school, students do not understand the track they have "chosen."

Choice and Guidance.   The preceding analyses demonstrate that choice is neither free nor informed in this track system. These conclusions are difficult to comprehend, in part because they come from such a general level of analysis. We do not know how or why the students are prevented from making free choices and from being aware of the significance of their choices. What do students know about tracking and about career opportunities? What alternatives do they perceive in their track choices? What constraints do they experience on their choices?

The guidance counselors have the responsibility for aiding and influencing students' track and career choices. Teachers do not have the time to give to this function. Parents, who may influence students' aspirations (Kahl, 1953), lack the knowledge or experience to inform students about choices. Cicourel and Kitsuse (1963, p. 46) reported that even upper-middle-class parents are "not informed about the substance or the importance of meeting college requirements." The working-class parents in Grayton, who have never attended college, must feel even less capable of providing adequate advice. Students' track and career choices must, therefore, be highly dependent on the school guidance counselors. I shall first describe some of the obvious features of the guidance system in this school and then turn to students' accounts of the guidance they received.

Obvious Features of Guidance: Vague Misdirection. Research in schools has tended to avoid describing the most salient features of guidance systems, because it is felt that these features are obvious. Yet some of these features give important indications about the kinds of guidance students receive.

Student handbooks are significant sources of information, particularly where the ratio of counselors to students is low (Grayton High School provided 4 counselors for 1800 students). The guidance department distributes the student handbook to all students in the school. We have already noted that the student handbook is vague about the structure of tracking (Chapter 3); it is, moreover, both vague and contradictory in describing the significance of each track. The handbook describes the college track as a means of preparing for college, but it also adds:

> Many of our pupils who do not plan to go to college choose this course because it furnishes them with the cultural background and the mental training that are so desirable for those entering other specialized fields.

The description of the general track is even more ambiguous.

> The general course with its diversified curriculum has a two-fold purpose. For those pupils who plan to enter employment immediately after graduation, it provides training in many specific fields. For others who have the opportunity for further education, it offers the preparation needed for admission to many specialized higher institutions of learning.

This kind of information certainly does not offer much assistance to a student trying to choose between tracks. Both tracks appear to offer the same options. We can certainly understand how students might confuse "specialized higher institutions of learning" with colleges. The phrasing is obviously confusing—if not deliberately misleading.

Other sources of information are available, but they are difficult to obtain. The guidance department possesses a small collection of college catalogues and vocational guidance books. The collection is kept in the lobby of the guidance suite, and rules prevent its removal from this location. This location limits access to the material, for the lobby is small, and only students whom teachers trust are granted passes to visit the guidance lobby. The open, public character of this lobby means that students can have no privacy as they use this material. I once observed a teacher teasing a general-track student because the student was perusing a college catalogue, and students report similar occurrences. Furthermore, guidance counselors rarely inform students that they could receive such information on their own. Even many college-track students do not realize that they could obtain copies of college catalogues.

Although we cannot infer the intent of these features of the guidance system, the net effects are clear. Students have little direct access to information about post–high school education and careers, and exploration of alternatives is discouraged. Therefore students are highly dependent on the guidance counselors for information and advice.

My own experience in interviewing the guidance counselors sheds further light on the way they provide guidance. Although the counselors appeared open in those interviews, the information they provided was vague, evasive, and misleading (see Chapter 3). This does not necessarily imply that this is the way they respond to students. But it does indicate that, when they feel it is useful to do so, they are capable of delivering long monologues that are vague, evasive, and misleading. As we shall see later, they sometimes use this capacity to considerable advantage when dealing with angry parents.

These observations do not describe the kind of guidance students receive. They do, however, illustrate how some potential sources of guidance are not used to communicate clear information effectively to students. These observations also delineate the context in which guidance is given and suggest a recurrent pattern of vagueness and evasiveness. Furthermore, in spite of the limited number of guidance staff, this pattern tends to provide students with few direct sources of information and to encourage students' dependence on the guidance counselors for information.

Student Experiences with Guidance. In describing their track choices and track changes, most students emphasize the guidance counselors' influence on their decisions, an influence that apparently operates in two distinct ways:

1. *Controlling Information*

Students require a great deal of information to make their track and career decisions, and the guidance counselors are responsible for providing them with this information. But, as noted earlier, the counselors are also responsible for advising students to choose the tracks and careers most appropriate to their ability. Students' accounts suggest that these two responsibilities —informing and advising—interact so that counselors provide a student with the kind of information that they judge to be most appropriate to the student's ability.

Students need to know the significance of choosing a foreign language in seventh grade, but the guidance counselors do not inform all students about this aspect of tracking. Therefore, some of the students who chose noncollege tracks in junior high did so without realizing it. Several students reported that they decided not to take a foreign language because they were not interested in traveling to foreign countries or because they preferred to learn typing. They were not aware that this choice also meant that they would receive inferior mathematics and English classes. "No one helped me decide. I just took typing because I wasn't interested in languages," reported a bright business-track girl. A general-track boy sadly sighed, "I just wish someone had told me how much better the courses were if you chose a language."

Yet the guidance counselors did not withhold this information from all students. Some students reported that they originally chose not to take a language in seventh grade, but a guidance counselor contacted them, informed them of the importance of taking a language, and advised them to do so. The account by a college-track girl began the same as the accounts of the noncollege-track students, "I really didn't have any interest in a foreign language. But," she went on, "then the guidance counselor called my parents and said I really should enroll in the foreign language course because I had good college potential." The guidance counselors did disseminate information about tracking to some students, but they did it selectively. They gave information to students who they felt needed the information.

Students also need to know the educational requirements for their aspired careers. Those who had wanted to be nurses, accountants, or engineers discovered too late that their aspired occupations required a college education. Although the counselors had been negligent in informing these noncollege-track students, several college-track students reported that they had decided to remain in their track because counselors had told them of the importance of college for their aspired careers.

A working-class student's prospects for college partially depend on financial considerations. Guidance counselors informed some college-track students about the possibilities of financial aid. Yet several noncollege-track students noted that they had switched out of college track because they could not afford college. The counselors had not informed them of scholarship and loan programs. Because some kinds of financial aid (e.g., NDEA) are available to anyone admitted to college, regardless of grades, the counselors' negligence precluded college opportunities for these students.

The choice to aspire to college is a risky decision for working-class students. A working-class student may fear that if he fails in his bid to attend college (through failure to be admitted or through lack of finances), his college preparation will have diminished his vocational preparation and his job chances. A college-track student, who had been making good grades, reported that he had gone to his counselor to switch to a curriculum that would prepare him for a clerical job in case he could not afford college. The counselor dissuaded him from the change, arguing that the college-track curriculum would be good preparation for a job, even if he did not attend college. Yet several noncollege-track students reported that, when they wanted to change to college track, the counselor dissuaded them from this by arguing that they would receive better preparation in the business or general tracks.

When noncollege-track students ask if they are receiving preparation for college, the counselors reassure them that the general track offers "a good general education for further education." Thus I find in the interviews, as I did in the questionnaires, many noncollege-track students believing that they can go to college. "My counselor advised that I change to the general track because it would be easier. He said my chances would still be very good for going to college." Students repeatedly explain that they are happy to be in a noncollege track, because it is "an easy way to get into college." These students realize that teachers regard them as inferior to college-track students, but, in the words of one student, "I don't have to put up with that very long, and I'll still get to go to college like they do."

To hear the general-track students express their impossible expectations was depressing, but none was more moving than a recent graduate of the lower general track who said, in an August interview, that he planned to enroll in Boston University the next month. He had not taken the courses required by colleges; he had not taken any admissions tests or filled out any admissions forms. He did not know anything about such things. He just knew that registration was being held next month, and he thought he would "just go down there and sign up."

The guidance counselors are responsible for providing students with information and advice. In actual practice, however, information and advice become related so that *students are provided with the kind of information that will ensure that the counselor's advice is chosen.* We might be tempted to rationalize this practice by saying that the counselors' decisions are in the best interest of the students and society because they are meritocratic, but the analyses in Chapter 4 demonstrate that this is not the case, and, even if it were, such deception is unwarranted. We might be tempted to doubt the accounts of these students, but it is all too clear that they are basing their hopes and plans upon patently false information.

2. *Coercion*

The selective presentation of information is a very effective means of influencing choice. It is easy and does not involve unpleasant situations. Occasionally, however, it is not adequate, and in these cases, the guidance counselors resort to blatant coercion. There are two kinds of situations which require coercion: coercing downward track changes and preventing upward track changes.

Most noncollege-track students begin in a college track but change tracks after doing poorly. Generally, they report that they had done poorly in only one or two courses in a single year. But this seems to have been sufficient cause for switching students out of college tracks. Nine general-track students report that they did not want to change out of the college track, but the guidance counselor insisted and made them change.

We have noted that students do not move up in track, particularly from noncollege to college tracks. This implies that students either do not desire or are not allowed upward track changes. As we have seen, many noncollege-track students do not desire to switch into a college track, because they are uninformed about the significance of tracking. Yet five students in the interview sample (one in business track and four in general track) attempted to transfer to a college track. All had originally been in the college track, and all but one tried to transfer back to the college track during their first year in the noncollege track. Each had found the noncollege track "too easy" and boring, and each expressed confidence that he could do college-track work if given a second chance.

The meeting with the guidance counselors regarding a track change was quite a fateful event in the lives of these students, and they remembered it vividly. While gathering data (copying the school record material), I had the opportunity to overhear two such meetings. My own impressions are consistent with the students' accounts, and I shall use both perspectives in describing the meetings.

The guidance counselors seem to have worked out strategies for persuading students to switch to, or remain in, a noncollege track. The main strategies in both cases are to disparage the student, stressing his lack of ability or his lack of motivation, and then to emphasize that the student's own behavior has made the counselor's decision inevitable. When the counselor begins talking to the student about his track placement, the student is already aware that his performance did not match the teacher's standards, a fact his teacher has probably stressed over the previous year. What may be less clear to the student is that the low evaluation is entirely his own responsibility. The counselor tries to impress this upon the student, by citing supportive evidence from the student's cumulative record and test scores. Occasionally, the counselor will suggest that even teachers who have given the student acceptable grades have had doubts about the student's capacity (the term "overachiever" is commonly used). In the case of students attempting to move up in track, the counselor ignores good grades in noncollege tracks, for those are "easy courses," and he focuses on average or below-average grades, even in nonacademic courses: "You only got a C in typing. How do you expect to pass in college-track courses?" Even the most self-assured student has some doubts about his ability, and the counselor's words, along with the authoritativeness of his position, are generally effective for eliciting a sense of inferiority in the student.

The guidance counselor's second step is to conclude that the student's poor performance indicates that he belongs in a noncollege track. This inference is not inevitable. There are many possible ways to respond to poor performance—changing teachers or teaching style, diagnostic testing, remedial homework, or tutoring—but a track system presents one overwhelmingly "logical" administrative solution, that is, to assume that poor performance indicates low competence and then reclassify the student to an "appropriate" track. This solution follows so directly from the track structure that none of the students ever think to question it.

This strategy is highly effective. To students wishing to switch back to college track, the counselors may suggest that the decision be postponed a bit longer. Such delays strengthen a subsequent argument that "you've missed too much college track material" and provide more time for boredom and apathy to set in. A student who had once attempted to switch back to college track finally "decided that I didn't care." Another said that "it was too much hassle. I'm just too lazy to make it in college track." The desire to switch tracks is further attenuated by students' misconception that noncollege tracks offer preparation for college.

Parents rarely became involved in track changes. Because the parents generally have not gone far in school, they often feel that the guidance counselors know more about educational matters, and they just go along with the decision. Furthermore, parents often do not understand the implications of the track system. "You'll still end up in college if you really work hard," a father told his daughter. She could not make him understand the importance of the track change, and so he would not support her.

But even when parents support a student's efforts, they are not very effective, largely because of the educational difference between parents and counselors and the way that the counselors use this difference. This difference creates an important difference in status between working-class parents and the middle-class counselors. Although the counselors often come from the same social background as the parents, their superior education, their professional job, and their higher income (and obviously more expensive clothes) clearly define a large difference between the successful counselors and the parents (and students) who are failures. Beyond the obvious status differences, the counselors have far greater facility with words than the parents, who have difficulty in finding the right words for this situation. In contrast, the counselors are invariably articulate. They push their verbal fluency to the fullest in these circumstances, using the biggest and most technical words possible and talking at considerable length. I have already noted this capacity in my own interviews with the counselors. Their technique is effective in dissuading parents from further protests.

Free versus Informed Choice.   These findings are disturbing, for they disabuse us of the widespread faith in education's responsiveness to choice. Parents and educators express great confidence in the importance of choice in determining student careers. Even some social scientists who are thought to be skeptics have accepted this view. Jencks concludes his overview of the tracking literature by stating "the evidence we have reviewed suggests that the existing system of curriculum choice is . . . . more heavily influenced by what students say they want than by anything else (Jencks et al., 1972, p. 37).

But Jencks's conclusion is not the only interpretation that can be given to his data. Jencks bases his conclusion on two statistics from the Coleman Report: "Ninety percent of those in the college curriculum said they wanted to go to college. Sixty-two percent of those in other tracks said they did not want to go to college" (*ibid.,* p. 34). He is impressed by the large size of these percentages, even though the latter statistic indicates that 38% of noncollege-track students have aspirations inconsistent with their preparation! This is less of a discrepancy than in Grayton, where 60% of noncollege-track students expected to attend college. The average school in the Coleman sample may be less extreme than Grayton, but the Coleman sample reveals the same pattern as Grayton. Many schools across the country permit—and perhaps encourage—students to hold unrealistic aspirations.

Jencks is aware of the possibility that students' choices may have been molded. In discussing these statistics, he concedes that what appears to be free choice may only show that students have "adapted their tastes to reality once the school authorities had defined reality for them" (*ibid.*, p. 34). This suggests that Jencks even has some doubts about whether the 62% of the noncollege-track students made free and informed choices. Unfortunately, Jencks's data do not allow him to do more than speculate on this possibility.

I have shown that guidance counselors do mold choices by the information they provide and withhold. Furthermore, this chapter has shown that the choices made by parents and students are not likely to be *free* and *informed* choices. We have seen that these working-class parents and students lack information about tracking and about college, and Cicourel and Kitsuse (1963) have demonstrated that this is also true for upper-middle-class parents and students. Given this lack of information, parents and students are dependent on school guidance counselors to provide them with both advice and information. What are the vocational options of the various tracks? What are the risks of not taking vocational training? Is the student a good candidate for the academic demands of college? Is the student likely to receive financial aid for college? Parents and students must ask these difficult questions, and their choices will be influenced by the answers they receive from the guidance counselors. Because these parents and students lack independent sources of information on these points, they are trapped in a "Catch-22" situation: choice before guidance is not informed, choice after guidance is not free.

Like much of the religious writing on free will, the educational literature on track and vocational choice seems to consider choice as an individual attribute that students bring to school. The quote from Jencks at the beginning of this chapter implies that students' choices are derived from personality attributes like self-esteem. But I have shown that their choices are not immutable attributes or attitudes. They are based on their perception of reality and their assessment of their chances for various opportunities. Guidance counselors play an important role in the formation of these choices; therefore, students' choices are by no means independent of the counselors' choices for the students. As social scientists, we would like to separate out statistically the independent influence of students' choices on their track placements, but a student's choice, independent of the counselor's advice and information, has no significance.

This is not to deny significance to students' beliefs that they chose their tracks! Their belief is important, for it indicates that they are convinced of the legitimacy of their placements. Offering students the illusion of choice is an effective means of enlisting their commitment to a system .which offers them few real advantages.

But choice cannot be measured by such beliefs, any more than it can be explained by individual attributes. I have shown that choice is the result of the complex interaction between the student and the school, and it must be measured in terms of the real options the students are offered, the information they are given about their options, and the degree to which they are permitted to choose options the counselors consider ill advised. The belief in choice creates perceived legitimacy, but it insidiously undermines opportunity and leads to ultimate disappointment.

NOTES

1. These breakdowns are not shown in Table 3.5.
2. Because this question is asked after a question about the student's aspirations, it is clearly asking students about realistic expectations rather than vague hopes.

Chapter 7
The Stratification of
Socialization Processes[1]

One way that stratification systems maintain and perpetuate themselves is by socializing people differently in different strata (see Clausen, 1968; Kohn, 1969). Because tracking is a stratification system in an institution explicitly committed to socialization, the study of tracking can help us understand how stratification influences socialization. This and the following chapters investigate the effects of school stratification (i.e., tracking) on student socialization.

The problem of perpetuating a stratification system is particularly difficult when its placements are not based on its presumed criteria. The Grayton track system is such a case. This chapter turns the tables on the concept of selection. It has been shown that educational selection is not based on ability; this chapter asks to what extent ability is influenced by educational selection. A selection system presumably gains its legitimacy by basing selections on personal attributes, but, lacking this, can the selection system create its own legitimacy by molding personal attributes to fit its selections?

Bowles and Gintis (1973) have speculated on the ways that stratification systems socialize their members, though their speculations are based on little data, and they assume that stratification precludes mobility. But we have seen that tournament selection encourages certain kinds of mobility, and we may expect that it might foster distinctive forms of socialization.

Previous research has been contradictory on the effects of tracking (see comprehensive reviews by Otto, 1950; Goodlad, 1960; NEA, 1968; Heathers, 1969; Findley and Bryan, 1971). One major fault has been its neglect of structural aspects of tracking. Previous research selected track systems for study without considering the particular structure of the system or the student body's social composition. Yet a track system that separates students minimally (e.g., in only one course) is likely to have fewer effects than one more extensively stratified. Furthermore, because track placements tend to reflect social class and racial differences, their effects cannot easily be separated from the effects of social background in most studies (see Hollingshead, 1949; Rist, 1970; Schafer and Olexa, 1971).

This study avoids these pitfalls by selecting a track system with distinctive structural characteristics. The track system is highly stratified and operates in a socially homogeneous community. This selection decreases the potential influence of social class and racial differences and increases the potential influence of tracking for differentiating students, enabling us to discover if tracking can have any influence independent of social class and racial differences. Furthermore, my extensive description of the social structure of this track system will help us understand the relationship between this structure and socialization outcomes.

This study also avoids two other shortcomings in previous

tracking research: its tendencies to look at very short-term changes (one year or less) and to investigate only mean gains and losses. This study investigates changes over a period of two years and performs several kinds of analyses of change.

The Dependent Variable.   Most studies of the effects of tracking use achievement test scores as the dependent variable, for such tests tap the specific skills appropriate to a particular year of schooling. Yet the narrowness of these tests can lead to problems in analyzing score changes. I found that the SCAT (School and College Ability Test) was apt to lead to a floor effect, because each of the lower tracks had a mean in the bottom quartile of the test. Since the various standardized tests of achievement and ability are highly correlated and similar in content, this analysis uses IQ rather than achievement test scores as the dependent variable. IQ test scores are likely to be even more reliable than achievement test scores, and changes in IQ scores are even more impressive, for IQ performance has been shown to be quite stable over time (Bloom, 1964, p. 64).

The Grayton school system administered the Otis IQ test to all students in the spring of their eighth and tenth grades. I was given access to the school records which contained these scores and students' track placements. This chapter reports the longitudinal analysis of the eighth and tenth grade IQ scores for one class of students (class of 1971) in Grayton high school ($n = 457$).

The Analysis.   This analysis is in two parts. The first part deals with the magnitude of individual change in the Grayton track system. It proceeds from an analysis of net gains to detailed investigations of individual change, tracking as the cause of such change, and the magnitude of tracking's effect. The second part takes a very different approach than Jencks and others. It focuses on changes on the group level, that is, on how individuals change in relation to others in their track and how students are socialized within each track.

I shall begin the analysis at the gross level, as Jencks does, and consider schoolwide change. The schoolwide mean on the eighth grade test is 102, and the mean on the tenth grade IQ test is 100. Thus, students do slightly worse, on the average, on the tenth grade test than on the eighth grade test, but the change is not pronounced.

Yet looking at the mean IQs for each track, we note a different pattern (see Table 7.1). The mean IQs decrease only in the three noncollege tracks. The two college tracks have mean increases. Furthermore, though not all these changes are statistically significant,[2] their magnitude is more pronounced than the schoolwide change. Clearly, IQ scores change in different directions in the college and noncollege tracks. This observation suggests that the net schoolwide decrease may signify nothing more about the school than that fewer students are in college than noncollege tracks. The important changes are in the individual tracks. A schoolwide analysis like Jencks's obscures more than it reveals.

Individual Changes. We have been looking at changes at the aggregate level of a track. Mean changes can be deceptive, for they may not accurately reflect the direction or amount of individual changes. We should look at individual score changes to get a better idea of the effect of tracking on IQ change. Table 7.2 presents the amount of IQ change individuals experienced in

TABLE 7.1.   MEAN IQ IN EIGHTH AND TENTH GRADES BY TRACK*

Track	Eighth Grade	Tenth Grade	N
Upper college	123	127	12
Lower college	107	109	151
Upper general	104	102	17
Business	99	95	208
Lower general	97	93	69

*This chapter alters the listed sequence of the noncollege tracks so that they are ranked in order of mean IQ rather than by name. This change clarifies the relationships between track and IQ.

TABLE 7.2. IQ CHANGE BY TRACK

IQ Change			Track		
	Upper College (%)	Lower College (%)	Upper General (%)	Business (%)	Lower General (%)
Increase 10+ points	33.3	12.6	0.0	1.9	4.3
Increase 4–9 points	8.3	25.2	17.6	10.6	4.3
No change	41.7	39.1	58.8	34.6	39.1
Decrease 4–9 points	0.0	15.9	11.8	38.0	40.6
Decrease 10+ points	16.7	7.3	11.8	14.9	11.6
Total	100.0	100.0	100.0	100.0	100.0
Number of cases	(12)	(151)	(17)	(208)	(69)

χ^2 = 79.2 with 16 df

Gamma = −.38

each track. Students' scores in the noncollege tracks clearly tend to decrease and those in the college tracks tend to increase. If one excludes students whose scores do not change by more than 3 points, fewer than one-quarter of the changes depart from this hypothesis (69 of 284 students). This tendency is even true for changes of 10 points or more (23 college-track students and 7 noncollege-track students increased by 10 points; 13 college-track students and 41 noncollege-track students decreased by 10 points).

These findings are striking, particularly since they are working against "regression to the mean." Since track placement is highly correlated with IQ scores ($r = .47$), it is quite possible that some of the initial low scores in the noncollege tracks and the initial high scores in the college tracks may systematically regress toward the mean because of measurement error. This means that the observed findings occur despite regression to the mean, and the tracking effects are likely to be stronger than this table indicates!

When the relationship of track and IQ is broken down by IQ quintile (Table 7.3), it can be seen unambiguously that the same relationship exists between track and IQ change at very different levels of IQ (gammas range from $-.45$ to $-.56$, except in the lowest IQ quintile, which exhibits a floor effect). The results emphatically refute regression to the mean as an explanation. Regression to the mean suggests that high-scoring individuals would be likely to decrease on a second test, but top-quintile (IQ = 114+) students are more likely to *increase* if the student is in college track (40% increase; 19% decrease). Regression to the mean suggests that low-scoring individuals would be likely to increase, but noncollege-track students in the second lowest quintile are much more like to *decrease* than to increase (53% decrease, 13% increase). Track clearly has a stronger effect than regression to the mean. When the two work in the same direction, the results are even more striking. Of the top-quintile noncollege-track students, 76% (16 of 21) decreased in IQ, and none increased.

This table shows unambiguously that the relationship between track and IQ change is not due to, but, indeed, is in spite of,

TABLE 7.3. IQ CHANGE BY TRACK CONTROLLING FOR INITIAL IQ

	Track				
IQ Change	Upper College (%)	Lower College (%)	Upper General (%)	Business (%)	Lower General (%)
Highest quintile IQ					
Increase 10+ points	33.3	18.2	0.0	0.0	0.0
Increase 4–9 points	8.3	21.8	0.0	0.0	0.0
No change	41.7	40.0	50.0	20.0	33.3
Decrease 4–9 points	0.0	7.3	0.0	33.3	33.3
Decrease 10+ points	16.7	12.7	50.0	46.7	33.3
Total	100.0	100.0	100.0	100.0	100.0
Number of cases	(13)	(55)	(2)	(15)	(6)
				$\chi^2 = 31.7$; 16 df	Gamma = −.56
Second highest quintile IQ					
Increase 10+ points	0.0	11.1	0.0	2.2	0.0
Increase 4–9 points	0.0	25.0	16.7	6.5	0.0
No change	0.0	27.8	50.0	19.6	25.0
Decrease 4–9 points	0.0	27.8	16.7	52.2	62.5
Decrease 10+ points	0.0	8.3	16.7	19.6	12.5
Total	0.0	100.0	100.0	100.0	100.0
Number of cases	(0)	(34)	(6)	(46)	(8)
				$\chi^2 = 18.8$; 12 df	Gamma = −.45
Middle quintile IQ					
Increase 10+ points	0.0	12.5	0.0	2.2	8.3

Increase 4–9 points	0.0	28.1	40.0	0.0	0.0	
No change	0.0	43.8	60.0	33.3	58.3	
Decrease 4–9 points	0.0	12.5	0.0	44.4	33.3	
Decrease 10+ points	0.0	3.1	0.0	20.0	0.0	
Total	0.0	100.0	100.0	100.0	100.0	$\chi^2 = 37.7$; 12 df
Number of cases	(0)	(32)	(5)	(45)	(12)	Gamma = −.48

Second lowest quintile IQ

Increase 10+ points	0.0	0.0	0.0	0.0	4.0	
Increase 4–9 points	0.0	31.6	0.0	18.2	0.0	
No change	0.0	47.4	100.0	38.6	25.0	
Decrease 4–9 points	0.0	21.1	0.0	34.1	54.2	
Decrease 10+ points	0.0	0.0	0.0	9.1	16.7	
Total	0.0	100.0	100.0	100.0	100.0	$\chi^2 = 21.1$; 12 df
Number of cases	(0)	(19)	(2)	(44)	(24)	Gamma = −.49

Lowest quintile IQ

Increase 10+ points	0.0	11.1	0.0	3.4	5.3	
Increase 4–9 points	0.0	22.2	0.0	19.0	15.8	
No change	0.0	44.4	50.0	48.3	52.6	
Decrease 4–9 points	0.0	22.2	50.0	25.9	21.1	
Decrease 10+ points	0.0	0.0	0.0	3.4	5.3	
Total	0.0	100.0	100.0	100.0	100.0	$\chi^2 = 3.0$; 12 df
Number of cases	(0)	(9)	(2)	(58)	(19)	Gamma = −.04

regression to the mean. It also shows that track affects IQ change in the same way at very different levels of IQ.

The Magnitude of the Tracking Effect.   The foregoing analysis, having shown that a relationship between track and IQ change exists independent of the initial level of IQ, had nonetheless, two shortcomings. First, it did not ascertain the magnitude of the tracking effect on IQ. Second, track is related to other factors that might be influencing the relationship of track to IQ change.

A regression analysis enables us to investigate both issues. In a regression equation of tenth grade IQ on eighth grade IQ and track placement (dichotomized into college vs. noncollege track), track explains 5% of the variance. If sex, social class, teacher recommendation, and SCAT verbal and mathematics scores are added into the regression, they all explain less than 4% more, and track placement still explains 4%. By adding these variables, we have reduced tracking's explanatory power by only 1%. Tracking clearly has a statistically significant ($p < .001$) effect independent of these other factors.

Beta weights, probably the best indication of the relative influence of each of these factors, are shown in Table 7.4. Tracking is clearly the most important factor for explaining the variance of tenth grade IQ not explained by eighth grade IQ.

In a personal communication (July, 1973), Jencks commented that this beta for tracking (.27) is about three times the coefficient in the sample of roughly 100 Project Talent high schools that he studied. As he notes, "this suggests that the effects of tracking may be unusually strong in . . . (this) school for some reason." This result validates the initial presupposition of this study; that is, that an analysis of the average effects of school factors obscures the genuinely important influences that occur in some schools. By

TABLE 7.4.   BETA WEIGHTS IN THE REGRESSION ON TENTH GRADE IQ

Eighth grade IQ	.71	Sex	.11
SCAT mathematics	.05	Social class	−.05
SCAT verbal	.02	Track	.27
Teacher recommendation	.01		

selecting a setting for which there were good structural reasons for expecting school effects to be unobscured by social class factors, this study indeed found that the effect of tracking can be much greater than Jencks's results had predicted. Furthermore, this study found that the influence of tracking is greater than, and largely independent of, the combined influence of teacher's recommendation, sex, and social class background.[3]

Group Level Changes.   Thus far I have been discussing changes in the magnitude of IQs. The mean IQs, the differences in individual IQs, and the regression equations all deal with the magnitude of IQs. Although these analyses have been more thorough than previous tracking research in analyzing the magnitude of change by different procedures, these analyses are merely an extension of the only perspective the tracking literature has ever taken.

But if tracking is seen as a form of stratification, and tracks are seen as discrete social groups, then the tracking process may be seen as a socialization of individuals relative to the group as a whole. Such a perspective calls for group level analyses.

The simplest descriptive measure of the relationship of an individual to a group is a measure of group dispersion such as variance. The variance of the IQs in a track is particularly relevant, for tracks are presumably composed of groups homogeneous in IQ. The tracking literature says nothing about the subsequent changes in IQ dispersion within a track, but clearly, such changes might be quite revealing about the socialization accomplished by tracking.

Table 7.5 shows the variances of eighth and tenth grade IQs for each track. The eighth grade IQ variances in the three noncollege tracks are quite similar, but the upper college track (which is also the smallest track) has a much smaller variance, and the lower college track has a larger variance. This suggests that the upper college track may be selected with a high concern for homogeneity, and the lower college track with a lesser concern for homogeneity.

But the most striking patterns in this table are the variance

TABLE 7.5.   IQ VARIANCES IN EIGHTH AND TENTH GRADE BY TRACK

Track	Eighth Grade	Tenth Grade	N
Upper college	23	48	12
Lower college	109	165	151
Upper general	96	94	17
Business	95	82	208
Lower general	87	78	69

changes between the eighth and tenth grades. The IQ variances
in the two college tracks markedly increase, but those in the three
noncollege tracks decrease. The increase in variance in the lower
college track is very significant by Hartley's test for homogeneity
of variance ($p < .01$; cf. Winer, 1962), and the decrease in variance
in the middle noncollege track is also significant ($p < .05$). Although the other changes are not large enough to be significant
(owing to the small number of students in these tracks), the
pattern of these changes is obvious. The changes in the variance
are much more dramatic than the changes in the means. The IQs
in the two college tracks become markedly more differentiated,
and the IQs in the three noncollege tracks become more
homogenized.[4, 5]

Interpreting IQ Changes: Myths and Misinterpretations.   What do IQ
changes signify? Psychologists who developed the IQ test intended that it measure "intelligence," and some psychologists
have continued to promote this interpretation (Eysenck, 1971;
Herrnstein, 1971). More cautious psychologists have admitted
the limitations of the IQ test, recognizing that it predicts only
likelihood of success in the current educational system (Wechsler,
1958). An indication of the difficulty psychologists have had in
defining intelligence can be seen in the definition that Professor
Boring made famous: "intelligence is what the test tests." What
test psychologists ignore in this operational definition is that we
have an intuitive understanding of the concept of intelligence
that the test may not measure at all.

Literally, the items in IQ tests are selected because they correlate with students' later school success; therefore, the IQ score derives its meaning, not from measuring intelligence, but from predicting future school success. If school selection were based on intelligence, then IQ tests predicting success in that system would measure intelligence. But a plethora of sociological research has shown that school selection is based on social class and racial differences at least as much as on measures of intelligence (Hollingshead, 1949; Sexton, 1961; Rist, 1970; Schafer and Olexa, 1971), and I have shown that, even where social class and racial differences are absent, school selection is not based on indicators of intelligence (neither IQ nor teachers' ability rating; see Chapter 4). Therefore, we must suspect that real school selection systems do not provide the preconditions necessary for constructing tests that actually measure intelligence. IQ tests are likely to measure industry, attendance, social class, and race at least as much as they measure intelligence.

Obviously, an IQ test defined in terms of success in a social system must necessarily incorporate the biases of that social system. Some of testing's critics have complained about the biases of tests and called for better, culture-free tests. But these critics miss the point. The problem is not simply biased tests; it is the fundamental dilemma of constructing unbiased tests in a biased social system.

There are also fundamental problems in interpreting IQ scores, independent of the social context of testing. Tests cannot tap capacity but only performance, and performance is a function of many qualities besides ability, for example, motivation, habits, and test-taking practice (Wechsler, 1958). In addition, as Jencks has noted, whether a test measures intelligence or achievement is really a matter of our assumptions about students' preparation. "When everyone is equally well prepared, achievement tests become aptitude tests. When people are unequally prepared, aptitude tests become achievement tests" (Jencks et al., 1972, p. 56).

These arguments suggest that IQ does not measure a single individual trait, intelligence, but rather a collection of traits, some of which do not reflect intelligence: industry, attendance, social class, and race. They also suggest that IQ does not directly measure individual traits; rather, it represents a prediction of an individual's likely school success. This prediction reveals something about the individual, but it also reveals the schools' success criteria. Therefore, IQ measures the interaction between traits of individuals and traits of schools. If racial bias in schools would cease and schools awarded success equally to all racial groups, then new IQ tests would be needed that would not measure race-related traits.

Furthermore, IQ represents an average prediction for all students in all the various schools in the initial standardizing sample. Yet we must suspect that this net average may contain and conceal markedly different processes. My own results point out that the relationship between IQ and success (measured by either grades or college attendance) is quite different in college and noncollege tracks. Similarly, we might suspect that this relationship may differ in different schools, depending on the school's social class and racial composition, degree of racial bias, percentage of graduates admitted to college, and academic climate. In other words, IQ may predict success accurately in some tracks and some schools and may not predict it accurately in other tracks and other schools.

In fact, what IQ really predicts, quite literally, is a person's likelihood for school success if that person were to be placed in the hypothetical "average track" in the "average school" of the original standardization sample. This may approximate reality in some settings, but its relevance to a real individual in a real track in a real school is always uncertain. Obviously, an "average track" in an "average school" is a mythical entity. Therefore, IQ does not measure intelligence; it does not exclusively measure individual traits; and it does not even measure a prediction that is necessarily applicable to a real track in a real school. When test psychologists resort to defining IQ as "what the test tests," they are admitting that IQ is really an esoteric construct that has only a hypothetical referent.

This is not to say that the IQ score has no meaning at all, but rather that its meaning is hypothetical. There is sometimes a scientific value in knowing a person's rank on a hypothetical scale that applies to another setting and to a very different group of people. But such a ranking has a hypothetical referent, depending on a lot of improbable assumptions, and it has several possible interpretations. Scientific theory is often evolved by using such contrary-to-fact hypothetical thinking. For example, economists have constructed models which assume that consumers have complete information about alternatives, and yet we all (including economists) are aware of our limited knowledge about the products we buy. The assumption, though untrue, is useful for evolving theoretical hypotheses, but few economists would advocate, for example, that this assumption be used to prevent the FDA from regulating food and drug products.

Similarly, we may find some scientific value in assuming that all schools award success based solely on intelligence, that the same amount of success always accrues from a given level of intelligence, that all individuals are equally motivated and equally well prepared, and, therefore, that all variation in test scores is due to individuals' intelligence and to no other personal, social, school, or accidental characteristic. But these assumptions are not correct descriptions of reality. They are simplifying assumptions that scientists adopt to help them develop the IQ test. Contrary-to-fact assumptions can aid scientific endeavors, but we must remember that they are untrue, and there is great danger in applying them to the real world for making policy decisions. Psychologists find the IQ test useful in constructing comparison groups for experiments, but that is quite different from using them to define students' learning opportunities and life careers.

For the scientific uses of IQ tests, one may readily assume that IQ measures an accurate prediction for the school success of all individuals, and one may ignore unusual individuals (like "late learners") for general theories. Similarly, one may be willing to assume that the test measures a personal attribute of an individual. These assumptions are adequate for scientific hypotheses, which always imply the caveat: "all other things being the same." But this caveat, crucial for science, is not a condition anyone would like to impose on reality. We do not wish to impose on "late learners" that their learning rate remain the same, and we do not want racially biased schools to maintain their biases. Indeed, if part of the predictive power of IQ tests derives, not from their testing intelligence, but from their capacity to measure race-related variables in racially biased schools, then using IQ tests for making placements in other schools recreates the same bias in new situations. In this case, "all things being the same" would lead to the spread of racial bias.

These considerations are not meant to single out IQ tests as particularly invalid. On the contrary, the IQ test has a strong empirical tradition, being one of the best psychological tests ever developed.[6] The problem with IQ tests comes when this scale is misapplied to the real world and called "intelligence." IQ can be a useful instrument for scientific studies, but it is terribly abused when applied to policies which deprive people of opportunities and when described in popular magazine articles which advocate increased social inequality. Such practices may serve expedient or ideological purposes, but they ignore the hypothetical nature of IQ tests.

Interpreting IQ Changes: Socializing Social Identity.   The foregoing considerations do not mean that IQ has no significance in schools. On the contrary, over the course of the twentieth century, the IQ score has come to have tremendous importance to school staff. Although the foregoing considerations suggest that an IQ test may not represent anything real about an individual or his future school success, the IQ score itself has come to have an importance to school staff that ensures that it will have social implications. We see abundant evidence of this social importance in Grayton. IQ tests are administered every two years in the Grayton schools, and these scores are readily available to all school staff. We have already noted that guidance counselors and administrators place considerable importance on IQ scores, often referring only to IQ scores to explain a student's track placement. Teachers are encouraged to consult a student's IQ score to understand the

student's school performance. The head guidance counselor reported that many teachers consult these scores, and roughly half
the teachers I interviewed said that they know the IQ scores of
many of their students.[7] Thus many teachers go out of their way
to look up IQ scores, and they tend to remember (or think they
remember) these scores.

The potential importance of IQ scores is illustrated by an
extreme example described by the head guidance counselor. He
told of a teacher who seated the students in his classroom in rank
order of IQ from front to back of the room. Fortunately, this is
unusual, but teachers' statements about the importance of IQ
scores suggest that many teachers carry such a rank ordering in
their heads. Most teachers interviewed believe that the IQ score is
a good reflection of students' general ability to do well in school
and in life. They also believe it is their professional duty to consult
IQ scores. As one teacher noted:

> We are obliged as professionals to use the tools of the trade, and IQ
> tests are one of those tools. Whenever I have a new class, I go to IQ
> scores to look for the geniuses and the potential learning problems.

Of course, IQ scores do not diagnose learning problems or
inform teachers how to respond to students; they only affix an
evaluative label to students. The head guidance counselor was
merely amused at the practice of seating students by IQ rank; he
did not try to discourage this use. No one knows how to use the
scores, and, apparently, their use for making a seating chart is as
"professional" as any other. The only clear accomplishment of IQ
scores is to compare all students on a single rank-order scale.
Regardless of whether this gets converted into a seating chart or a
mental ranking, it constitutes an important evaluative label.

The clearest interpretation of IQ scores may, therefore, be in
terms of their social meanings. Regardless of whether IQ reflects
ability or motivation, IQ represents a social label that the school
values; and, as such, it is likely to affect the way a student is treated
by school personnel. According to the symbolic interactionists,

this social label is part of a person's social identity in the school system, and IQ changes, per se, constitute real changes in an individual's social identity. Even if IQ changes do not denote inner changes in the student's brain power or drive, they will be recognized and responded to by teachers as a change in social identity, and this constitutes a *socially real change.*

Furthermore, as my findings here imply (and as I shall note in more detail in Chapter 9), a student's IQ, along with the socialization requirements of the track structure, may determine how the student is subsequently socialized (e.g., noncollege-track students with high IQs are socialized for IQ decreases). These scores, which originally have only social meanings may, therefore, encourage changes in students' actual behaviors and perhaps even in their personal characteristics (see Rosenthal and Jacobson, 1968; Rubington and Weinberg, 1968; Mercer, 1973).[8]

The Stratification of Socialization.   The model of tracking as stratification suggests that track structure presents very different environments to students in different tracks. The analysis implies, moreover, that these different environments may be responsible for the two kinds of socialization processes observed; that is, that college tracks lead to differentiating processes and noncollege tracks lead to homogenizing processes. This perspective is strikingly similar to the types of socialization environments proposed by Stanton Wheeler:

> *homogenizing* settings that tend to reduce the relevance of prior experience for present adjustment . . . [and] *differentiating* settings [in which] authorities may urge recruits to give expression to the different backgrounds and interests they bring into the organization (Wheeler, 1966, p. 76).

Furthermore, like our analysis, Wheeler's examples suggest that upper status settings (e.g., liberal colleges) differentiate their members, but lower status settings (e.g., prisons, army training units) homogenize their members. Other examples of homogenizing socialization can be seen in studies of deprived people: the deviant (Sudnow, 1965); the sick (Scheff, 1966); and the poor (Piven and Cloward, 1971). In contrast, differentiating settings generally exist to serve those at the other end of the stratification hierarchy; human potential centers, hippie communes, psychoanalysis, and open education schools largely serve the upper middle class.

The stratification basis of socialization is also set forth by Melvin Kohn, who notes that:

> self-direction, in short, requires opportunities and experiences that are much more available to people who are more favorably situated in the hierarchical order of society; conformity is the natural consequence of inadequate opportunity to be self-directed (Kohn, 1969, p. 189).

My discovery of differentiating and homogenizing socialization patterns is quite similar to Kohn's distinction between self-direction and conformity. Even in a homogeneous, white, working-class school, this study finds that a track system can have these two different socialization effects.

How does the track system effect these two socialization processes? The possibilities are numerous. Do the noncollege tracks offer students a more homogeneous selection of courses; a narrower range of opportunities (in school or after graduation); lower teacher expectations (see Rosenthal and Jacobson, 1968); or peers who are less stimulating intellectually and/or motivationally? Each of these intervening variables may affect socialization, and each may be the result of the stratification properties of tracking. Furthermore, these processes may have analogues in societal stratification and lead to comparable socialization processes in society. The questions are intriguing, and we shall examine them further in Chapter 9.

Conclusion. The results of these analyses are based on only a single case, and this case has distinctive structural characteristics that heighten the potential effects of tracking. Yet this case study has led, not only to noting stronger effects, but also to discovering new kinds of effects. These findings compel us to reconceptualize tracking, not as a simple pedagogical technique, but as a stratification mechanism.

This, in turn, has implications for research. Rather than look at the effects of any and all forms of tracking in unspecified settings (as previous research has done), one must consider the specific track structure and the school's social composition. And rather than look only at simple additive effects, one must also investigate group level effects on the dispersion of scores. The latter finding is particularly damaging to previous research on school effects, because that research has often used statistical analyses that are not applicable if dispersion is not homogeneous throughout the scale, or, even more serious, if changes in dispersions are the main effects (e.g., Jencks et al., 1972).[9] My results demonstrate that most of the social science controversy about school effects has analyzed the issue on an excessively gross level, ignoring important features of the social process within schools.

Reconceptualizing tracking also leads to a very different assessment of its effects. Although previous research concludes that tracking has very small or mixed effects, my study concludes that tracking can have substantial effects if the school has a highly stratified track structure and that these effects are independent of initial ability, sex, race, or social class. It is all the more striking that the effects observed are IQ changes, for IQ has been shown to be stable in this age range.

The observed IQ changes are important not only because they may signify changes in student ability but also because they are socially valued and may affect students' education, track, and career opportunities. My findings suggest that the social structural properties of tracking lead to different socialization processes that have consequences on a socially important student attribute. The differentiation in the college tracks suggests that tracking may encourage students to realize their individual potential. The homogenization of the noncollege tracks implies that tracking may be channeling these students' intellects through a narrow funnel to a predetermined target level (see the appendix to this chapter). That this level is low makes the process particularly repugnant, but even if it were higher, hewing a group of individuals to some predetermined dimensions reflects a lack of responsiveness to individual abilities and needs. Certainly, such a process does not fit the school's goal of developing individual potential.[10]

APPENDIX: MODELING THE CHANGE PROCESS IN EACH TRACK

Thus far, I have analyzed the effects of tracking by looking at mean and variance changes. Regression modeling can provide another means of summarizing the change process by giving the best-fit equation for describing the data. Whereas means and variances describe gross changes, modeling by regression equations can provide a general description of the transformation process for individual scores, revealing who gains and who loses within each track. Furthermore, it can estimate the target to which noncollege-track IQ scores are being homogenized. Because these analyses are rather technical and do not substantially alter the conclusions of previous analyses, they have been relegated to this appendix.

My earlier regression analysis investigated the magnitude of tracking's effect as if tracking were equally influential in all tracks and influential in the same way in each. Yet an inspection of the mean and variance changes shows that different tracks have different impacts. We can get a better understanding of the change process in each track by constructing regression models for each track. These models enable us to look at the best linear description of the transformation of eighth grade IQs into tenth grade IQs in each track. Such an analysis presents a clear description by portraying only the general relationship and eliminating unusual (outlying) data.

Before proceeding to the analysis, let me pause to point out what can be discerned from such an analysis. The general form for a linear regression equation for any track would be $IQ10 = B(IQ8) + C$, where we are predicting the tenth grade IQ score ($IQ10$) from the eighth grade score ($IQ8$), B and C being constants derived from the regression analysis. The values of B and C describe the magnitude of change, and they also illuminate the process of change.

Table 7.6 shows the linear regressions for each track. Note that R^2 for each of these linear regressions is over .500, and each of the F tests is quite significant. These facts suggest that each equation is a good model of the actual distributions. Furthermore, Barlett's test for homogeneity of variance on the residual mean square reveals that each of these equations is an equally good explanation of the data (i.e., there is equal noise after removing the regression lines).

Surveying these equations, we see two distinct patterns. The three noncollege tracks have small Bs and large Cs ($B = .74$ and $C = 23$), but the two college tracks have B coefficients roughly equal to 1 and have small constants, Cs. Thus, the data confirm that the tracks that are similarly defined have similar effects on IQ, and we can speak of two processes: a noncollege-track process and a college-track process.

The regression equations for noncollege tracks describe a homogenizing process. Their equations are roughly $IQ10 = .74(IQ8) + 23$. Of course, this is consistent with the variance decrease already noted, but it also indicates that the variance decrease tends to affect all scores in the noncollege tracks. The regression analysis indicates that there is a general homogenization process that affects most IQ scores in the noncollege tracks.

TABLE 7.6   LINEAR REGRESSION EQUATIONS OF TENTH GRADE IQ ON EIGHTH GRADE IQ FOR EACH TRACK

Track	Equations	R^2	F Test Sig. Level
Upper college	$IQ10 = .96\ IQ8 + 5.2$	.62	.001
Lower college	$IQ10 = 1.03\ IQ8 - 1.6$	.71	.001
Upper general	$IQ10 = .75\ IQ8 + 24.5$	.58	.01
Business	$IQ10 = .74\ IQ8 + 22.3$	.63	.001
Lower general	$IQ10 = .73\ IQ8 + 22.3$	.52	.01

The significance of this equation can be understood by considering the alternatives. The mean and variance decreases observed in the noncollege tracks could have been due to changes in only a small part of the IQ scale. For example, net decreases in means and variances could occur if the highest scores decreased slightly and all others remained constant; if the highest scores decreased a lot and the lowest scores increased slightly; if the highest and lowest scores remained constant but the middle scores converged and decreased; and so forth. There are a plethora of possible ways in which those gross statistics could be produced. A painstaking analysis of Table 7.3 can reveal which of these possibilities is most likely, but it is difficult to summarize the findings of that large table.

The regression equation provides a summary of the general process that tends to happen to the scores in each of the three noncollege tracks. Not only is there a net decrease in variance in these tracks, but also there is a general tendency for all scores to converge. Furthermore, this equation points to the degree of convergence. It shows that a four-point IQ difference between two students in eighth grade is likely to be reduced to a three-point difference by tenth grade.

The regression equations for college tracks describe a "stay same" process. Their equations are roughly $IQ10 = 1.0(IQ8) + 0$. This says that insofar as tenth grade IQ is a function of eighth grade IQ in the college tracks, there will be no change. Of course, we know that there is a slight mean increase in IQ, and there is a substantial variance increase. We must, therefore, infer that these changes are not a function of original IQ but are rather, due to other factors (i.e., the residual unexplained by IQ8).

This equation, while not accounting for the gross variance increase, does say something important about it, namely, that the substantial variance increase in the college tracks is not due to a process of the rich getting richer and the poor, poorer. If the high scorers were the ones showing the biggest gains and the low scorers were the ones showing the biggest losses, then the B coefficient would have been greater than 1. Rather, the "stay same" equation that we observe for the college track shows that the variance increase is due to increases by both high and low scorers and decreases by both high and low scorers. Within the two college tracks, IQ changes are not due to advantages accruing to high initial IQ. (Since I lack eighth grade indicators of other student qualities and performances, I cannot say what factor is accounting for this variance increase.)

These regression models also enable me to solve each equation for the conditions when IQ10 is less than IQ8, that is, when IQ decreases. I find that IQ decreases in:

Upper college track	if IQ8 > 130 (rarely)
Lower college track	if IQ8 < 53 (never)
Upper general track	if IQ8 > 98
Business track	if IQ8 > 86
Lower general track	if IQ8 > 83

The solutions for the two college tracks explain few, if any, scores. But the solutions for the noncollege tracks are at least three points below the medians for these tracks, indicating that most students' scores decrease in the noncollege tracks and, conversely, that few scores increase. Scores in the noncollege tracks may, therefore, be homogenized to a low "target" level of IQ.

The analyses of the regression models confirm and extend my earlier analyses, indicating that IQ changes in the college tracks are not related to students' initial IQs. The college-track IQ changes do not represent a process of the high scores increasing and the low scores decreasing; rather, these changes are fairly independent of initial IQ. On the other hand, the regressions for noncollege tracks indicate that the previously observed IQ decreases and homogenization represent a general process within each noncollege track that tends to affect all students and that depends on a student's initial IQ. Students who score above the "target" tend to experience IQ decreases, and those below the "target" tend to experience increases, but the "target" is quite low. These regressions indicate not only a general homogenization process, but they also indicate that students' scores are homogenized to a rather low "target."

NOTES

1. This is an expanded version of a paper published in the *American Sociological Review* (Rosenbaum, 1975). This chapter is particularly indebted to the provocative paper by Light and Smith (1971).

2. The differences between the means for the middle and lower noncollege tracks are highly significant ($p < .001$). The differences in the means for the other tracks are not significant.

3. This analysis is a conservative indication of the effect of tracking. Regressing these variables on the *change* in IQ scores shows that tracking has an even larger influence. The beta weights are as follows:

Eighth grade IQ	−.24	Sex	.17
SCAT mathematics	−.05	Social class	−.05
SCAT verbal	.16	Track	.34
Teacher recommendation	−.08		

4. Although I have interpreted these findings as the effects of tracking, there is another possible explanation. Track placement could be interpreted as reflecting a teacher's prediction of a student's change in ability. According to this explanation, track does not *cause* the change in IQ; rather, track placement is the *result* of the teacher's prediction of IQ change. Thus, a teacher will place college-track ninth grade students in noncollege tracks the next year if he feels that these students will be unable to cope with the harder intellectual tasks required in the tenth grade (which will be tested on the tenth grade IQ test). But there are several problems with this interpretation.

   Although this interpretation does explain mean changes, it does very badly at explaining variance changes. This interpretation says that students are placed in the track most appropriate to their future IQ; therefore, this interpretation predicts decreasing variance for all tracks. Clearly, this cannot explain the marked variance increase in the lower college track. Insofar as this variance increase reflects a spreading down of scores, then those individuals should have been placed in a noncollege track; insofar as this increase reflects a spreading up of scores, then those individuals should have been placed in the upper college track. As we have seen, 23% of the lower-college-track scores do decrease four points or more, and more than one-third of these decreases are for individuals with IQs that would have placed them in a noncollege track in the first place (in the lowest 60% of IQ, less than 105). Similarly, 18% of the top-quintile lower-college-track students increase 10 points or more, and yet they are not placed in the upper college track. If the teachers are predicting a student's IQ changes, the predictions are either inaccurate or not being implemented.

But a more fundamental empirical problem is that the track structure does not allow a teacher to act on his prediction for noncollege-track students. If a teacher felt that a noncollege-track student would increase in IQ, he would put that student in the college track, and I would mistakenly count him as a college-track increase. But the track system does not permit this. Therefore, when I find relatively few increases in IQ in the noncollege tracks (fewer than 11%), this cannot be due to the reassignment of noncollege-track students who increase to college tracks, for upward reassignment is not possible. I am forced to conclude that the noncollege tracks do not stimulate many students to increase in IQ.

These considerations lead me to conclude that my interpretation that tracking causes the IQ changes is probably the best way to interpret these data.

5. Some readers may be concerned with the possible effects of measurement error on IQ test scores. Yet any compensation that I would make for test error would make no change in some of my findings and might strengthen others. As to

variance changes, I have noted that the observed variance is significantly different between eighth and tenth grades. Since

observed variance (8th) =
 actual variance (8th) + error variance
and
observed variance (10th) =
 actual variance (10th) + error variance,

and since the error variances at the two times are the same, then any significant difference in observed variance also reflects a significant difference in actual variance. Measurement errors have no influence on the variance change findings.

Could measurement error wipe out the observed individual and mean IQ changes? We assume that measurement error is random. We know that random error does not introduce consistent effects; rather it tends to obscure actual consistent effects. Thus, random error would be operating here to make the observed relationships appear *less* strong than they actually are (see footnote 8, below, for a critique of the use of "true scores").

6. The reliability and predictive validity of IQ tests are far better than those of most other psychological tests. IQ tests also tend to be a better predictor of future school success than the subjective professional judgments of teachers and counselors. As noted in Chapter 4, if any test or evaluation must be used for early permanent placements of students, the IQ test would be the most appropriate. Yet Chapter 4 suggests that the most appropriate test may not be the most likely to be used within a school, and this chapter indicates that IQ scores are so malleable that they cannot justify early permanent placements. As I shall conclude in Chapter 10, rather than pick the best test, which is still inadequate, for making early selections, schools must consider how necessary the selection is.

7. Interviews with teachers were not conducted with a random sample.

8. Recent educational research has devoted an enormous amount of energy to using statistical procedures for calculating the "true scores" on IQ tests (see Bloom, 1964; Jencks et al., 1972). The concern of these researchers is that the IQ test is not completely reliable, that is to say, that a second administration of the same or similar test does not produce the same score. This unreliability is attributed to what is called "measurement error," and educational researchers use statistical procedures to take account of this "measurement error" and find the "true score."

Actually, the relationships I discovered for observed scores are just as likely to hold for "true scores"; "measurement error" does not weaken my findings (see footnote 5, above). Moreover, my analysis of IQ indicates that "true scores" are irrelevant. The "true score" is a mathematical transformation to get to the underlying reality of what the test is measuring. But I have concluded that there is no simple, unambiguous reality that the test is measuring. The test is not measuring intelligence; it is not measuring individual traits; and it is not even measuring a real prediction. The test is measuring a prediction about students in a hypothetical situation. On the other hand, I have concluded that, although the IQ test does not have any real referent, the IQ score has acquired a real social meaning. Therefore, "correcting" the observed score into a "true score" actually takes us further away from reality.

The IQ scores written in the school records are statistically unreliable (e.g., if the test was administered again); but after they are recorded, the written numbers stay the same and are the scores that are important. They are the scores that teachers look at, that a teacher could use to seat students by, and that teachers use to judge a student's intelligence (intelligence in our common meaning of the term, not in the psychologists' esoteric, hypothetical meaning). The recorded scores are not a proxy for the "true scores," for the "true scores" have no real referent. The recorded scores are the only scores having an unequivocal meaning. They are the ones that create students' social identities. These are the scores that I used in my calculations, and my calculations show the effects of tracking on students' social identities.

9. For linear regression equations to be applicable, we "need to assume that the standard deviations (or variances) of the Ys for each X are the same regardless of the value of X. . . . This property of equal variances is referred to as *homoscedasticity*" (Blalock, 1960, p. 279). Jencks relies on path analyses for most of his conclusions, and path analyses require this assumption. Yet Jencks does not explicitly consider the homoscedasticity assumption or notice that it is violated in his data. My variance analyses throw his basic assumption into doubt.

10. These results also have important implications for the stability of track placements. Tables 7.3 and 7.5 show that bright noncollege-track students, whose placements are either ambiguous or incorrect, experience the greatest IQ decreases and thereby ratify and stabilize their noncollege-track placements. This will be discussed further in Chapter 9.

Chapter 8

Socializing Youth
for Social Inequality

Does tracking affect student's attitudes and behaviors? I have shown that the track system influences their IQ scores, but IQ scores reflect student attributes which are directly related to school. Students' attitudes and behaviors are far more pervasive than IQ and may be immune to the school's influence.

There are two reasons for believing that school might have no bearing on students' social attitudes and behaviors. The family is likely to exercise a crucial formative influence in socializing youth, and family social status is likely to label youth in such profound ways that the school's contribution might be relatively trivial in comparison (see Boocock, 1972, for a review of this literature). Hollingshead's classic study (1949) showed that high

school staff largely respond to students' social class back
in assigning track placements and other school privileges a
students' attitudes and behaviors are largely dependent or
background. The function of the school may merely be to ratify,
and to some limited extent, elaborate, the differences in social
background that youth bring to the school.

Peer pressures also tend to undermine the influence of the
school, as Coleman (1961) has shown. Coleman's survey demonstrates that students exhibit a high degree of consensus on attitudes, particularly on antischool attitudes, and that they consider a teacher's disapproval less important than maintaining
friendships with peers.[1] Coleman also observes that leading
crowds tend not to include the most academically oriented students, and that, indeed, they tend to be even more antagonistic to
academic values than the nonelites. He concludes that "the adolescent lives more and more in a society of his own" (*ibid.*, p. 312),
and this adolescent society operates in ways which undermine the
influence of the school. "Society is confronted no longer with a set
of *individuals* to be trained toward adulthood, but with distinct
social systems, which offer a united front to the overtures made by
adult society"(*ibid.*, p. 4).

Yet there are important issues that these studies do not consider. Hollingshead finds that differences in social background
have such blatant effects on the school's operation that he feels no
need to discuss the independent influence of school on students'
social attitudes and behaviors. As noted in Chapter 1, Hollingshead made this point so well that contemporary sociological
research has largely considered tracking's effects to be merely an
extension of the effects of social class background (see Sexton,
1961; Schafer and Olexa, 1971). Yet studying these issues in a
socially homogeneous school like Grayton allows us to consider
whether a school track system can affect students' attitudes and
behaviors in the absence of social class differences.

Likewise, without disputing Coleman's results, I will consider
some important issues which he did not analyze. Coleman found
that being a leader in activities was considered important for

status and popularity (Coleman, 1961, pp. 29, 44), but he did not ask whether school factors determine which students participate and lead in activities. Similarly, he showed the effect of friendships on values (*ibid.*, Chapter 7), but he did not ask whether school factors sway friendship choices. Finally, although Coleman sought to describe the social structure of the student subculture, he did not even mention the social structure of the school track system. I must take the next step beyond Coleman's investigation and ask whether tracking has any effect on friendship choices or on participation or leadership in school activities.

Tracking into Separate Societies.   Students were asked (on the questionnaire) what extracurricular activities they participate in (see Table 8.1). Although roughly half the students participate in activities, the percentage varies considerably in different tracks. The majority of students in most noncollege tracks do not participate in any extracurricular activities, but the majority of the college-track students do participate. Indeed, more than 80 percent of the upper-college-track students and more than 30 percent of the lower-college-track students participate in two or more activities, although fewer than 15 percent of noncollege-track students do so. Clearly then, whether or not a student participates in extracurricular activities is highly dependent on what track he is in.

Furthermore, those few noncollege-track students who do participate in extracurricular activities seem to be restricted to only certain activities. Of the general-track students in activities, 70% are in just two particular activities (athletics and band), and the majority of business-track students in activities are in just three particular activities (band, service club, and drama club). The members of the school publications, the student council, and the political clubs, and the officers of all the clubs come predominantly from the college tracks. Thus, a rather high degree of track separation is maintained, even among participants in extracurricular activities, and the influential clubs and leadership positions are available only to college-track students.

TABLE 8.1. STUDENTS IN ZERO, ONE, OR TWO EXTRACURRICULAR ACTIVITIES, BY TRACK

Number of Activities	Track					
	Upper College (%)	Lower College (%)	Upper Business (%)	Lower Business (%)	Upper General (%)	Lower General (%)
No activities	9	33	55	64	41	66
One activity	9	36	24	25	45	22
Two or more activities	82	31	21	11	14	12
Total	100	100	100	100	100	100
Number of cases	(11)	(75)	(41)	(44)	(22)	(41)

Of course, correlation does not signify causality, but students themselves report (in the interviews) that their track placements influence their participation and leadership opportunities. Some noncollege-track students (5 of 30) report that teachers discouraged them from participating in activities or from running for elective positions because of their track placement. Many students feel that informal social pressures prevented their participation. Many noncollege-track students (10 of 30) say that they did not attempt to participate in activities, because they felt that these were college-track activities, and they would feel uncomfortable and unwelcome; of those who did attempt to participate, many (8 of 20) found this to be true and dropped out of the activity. Most noncollege-track students (18 of 30) believe that their track placements restrict their opportunities for participation and leadership in school activities.

Tracking is also an important factor in determining peer group composition. The interviews asked students the track placements of their five best friends. Table 8.2 shows the number of respondents in each track choosing friends in their own track. More than half the respondents in each track have a majority of their friends in their own track. Furthermore, most of the friends not in one's own track area are in one's adjoining track. Table 8.3 shows the number of respondents in each track choosing friends in their own or the adjoining track.[2] Virtually all students choose a majority of their friends from their own or the adjoining track, and more than 70% of those in each track choose all five best friends from these tracks.

Again, one cannot be certain that this high correspondence denotes a causal relationship, but logic suggests that tracking does influence friendships. Students spend a great deal of time in school or in school-related activities. If tracking separates students from one another by classes during school hours and by extracurricular activities after school hours, then very little time is left for maintaining friendships with students in other tracks. Therefore, owing to time limitations alone, tracking is likely to influence friendship choices.

TABLE 8.2. NUMBER OF BEST FRIENDS IN THE SAME TRACK AS RESPONDENT, BY RESPONDENT'S TRACK

Number of Friends	Respondent's Track				
	Upper College (%)	Lower College (%)	Business (%)	Upper General (%)	Lower General (%)
One or two friends	0	7	20	17	7
Three friends	17	36	10	17	21
Four or five friends	83	57	70	66	72
Total	100	100	100	100	100
Number of cases	(6)	(14)	(10)	(6)	(14)

159

Students relate personal experiences which indicate other ways in which tracking influences friendship patterns. Friendships in the elementary grades tend to be based on neighborhood proximity, but when students come to the junior high schools, they encounter strong social pressures to select their friends according to track. One girl reports that, only a month after she arrived in the junior high school, her best friend began acting snobbishly, saying she was smarter, and soon stopped playing with her entirely. At the time, the friend was in the top level of the college track, and the respondent was in the third level of the college track. Even such a small difference in track placement had an important effect on their friendship. Another student reported that

> some of my friends were put into other levels of the college track and everybody found new friends, new groups, and didn't associate too much with kids in the other groups. By the time you got to ninth grade, you had a whole different set of friends and you were supposed to stay within that group. Well, you had to, really. Everybody had their little group and it is really hard to break into another one. They were little social cliques.

The school track placements become the new basis for formal and informal interaction; neighborhood friendships dissolve and track-based friendships supplant them.

These data do not contradict Hollingshead's or Coleman's findings, but they extend their contentions somewhat. Although Hollingshead holds that social class discrimination is the basis for the school's influence on students' participation, leadership, and friendships, my data indicate that the school's track system itself can have the same effects (in the absence of social class differences). Although Coleman finds that nonacademic values (such as popularity, attractiveness, and athletics) seem to influence students' access to some friendship groups, to some activities, and to leadership positions, my research suggests that one school factor also has an important influence. School track position is related to these social behaviors, and noncollege-track students report that

TABLE 8.3. NUMBER OF BEST FRIENDS IN THE SAME OR ADJOINING TRACK, BY RESPONDENT'S TRACK

| | Respondent's Track | | | | |
Number of Friends	Upper College (%)	Lower College (%)	Business (%)	Upper General (%)	Lower General (%)
One or two	0	0	10	17	0
Three	0	7	10	0	0
Four or five	100	93	80	83	100
Total	100	100	100	100	100
Number of cases	(6)	(14)	(10)	(6)	(14)

their social behavior is influenced by the way other people evaluate and treat them as members of a lower track.

Granted, family and peers exert important influences on students' social behaviors, but we have seen that school does so, too. The school affects formal school-related behavior, and it also affects informal behaviors in nonacademic realms. Furthermore, in contrast with Coleman's analysis, which considers the importance of peers in subverting school factors, my analysis points to the school factor of tracking (which Coleman did not consider) as actually constraining peer choices and thereby determining which peer pressures a student is exposed to.

Tracking and Social Evaluation.   As officially defined in Grayton and in the educational literature, tracking is an unimportant and reversible distinction based only on students' curricula preferences. The official definition plays down the importance of track distinctions, implying that all students are similar. Some students choose more academic paths and others choose nonacademic paths, depending on personal taste, but all students are basically alike and could change tracks if they wished (see Chapter 3). The official definition holds that tracking does not foster stereotypes or social prejudices. Being merely an unimportant pedagogical distinction, tracking is said to encourage students to perceive those in different tracks as fairly similar, except in terms of their personal taste for academic work. Of course, having seen how tracking affects students' social behavior, we might suspect that it also shapes their attitudes, particularly their attitudes toward one another. Do track placements, which are designed to have only educational implications, also take on implications for social evaluation?

This question is analogous to the question in the stratification literature—are people in different economic positions in society described and evaluated any differently by other members of society? Although there is no necessary relationship between wealth and social evaluation, the stratification literature indicates that peoples' perceptions and evaluations of others are swayed by the evaluated person's economic position. People with high incomes tend to receive positive social evaluations, those with low incomes tend to receive negative evaluations, and the stereotypes for each tend to be related to status criteria. For example, Warner and Lunt found that wealthy people in Yankee City were described as "aristocrats," and the poor were described as "lulus."

The interviews asked respondents to describe the students in each track. For the preceding reasons, and also because all students come from the same social background, we might expect that most respondents would say that students are all pretty similar. Furthermore, we might expect that if they offered distinctions, their distinctions would be related to the official definition of tracking. Thus they might say that college-track students are "academically oriented," "interested in college," or "want a job that requires college." But if administrators have succeeded in imparting the official definition of tracking as an open contest, then we would not expect students to say that students in different tracks differ in personal capacities.

My interviews reveal results quite discrepant from these expectations. More than three-quarters of the Grayton respondents provide stereotypes of the students in each track, and the stereotypes refer to personal capacities of the students (see Tables 8.4 and 8.5).[3] College-track students are characterized as smart or "brains" by more than half of those responding and as hard workers by more than a third, these descriptions being offered by a substantial number of respondents from each track. College-track students are also characterized as "snobs" and as "conformists" ("momma's kids," "brown nose") by one-sixth of the respondents.

The most common descriptions for noncollege students are the opposites of the preceding. They are described as unmotivated (or "lazy," "goof-offs," or "don't care about school") by more than half of the respondents, as negativistic (troublemaking or tough) by more than one-third, and as not very smart (or stupid) by more than one-quarter.

Although students accept some aspects of the official contest

TABLE 8.4. NUMBER OF RESPONDENTS OFFERING VARIOUS DES-
CRIPTIONS OF COLLEGE-TRACK STUDENTS BY RESPONDENT'S TRACK

	Respondent's Track	
Descriptions	College Track	Noncollege Track
Smart	9	13
Hard worker	7	8
Snob	1	7
Conformist	1	6
Total number of respondents	(15)*	(24)*

*Not all interviewees responded to question, and many respondents
offered more than one description.

definition of tracking (Chapter 6), they do not accept the administrative claim that students in different tracks are similar. Respondents show no reluctance to describe students in different tracks
in stereotypic terms. Furthermore, rather than describe students
in terms of their academic interests or vocational preferences,
they describe them in terms of personal capacities. In spite of its
official policy, tracking seems to contribute to the stereotyping of
students.

Tracking is not, however, solely responsible for these

TABLE 8.5. NUMBER OF RESPONDENTS OFFERING VARIOUS DES-
CRIPTIONS OF NONCOLLEGE-TRACK STUDENTS BY RESPONDENT'S
TRACK

	Respondent's Track	
Descriptions	College Track	Noncollege Track
Not very smart	1	7
Unmotivated	9	11
Negativistic	7	5
Total number of respondents	(14)*	(20)*

*Not all interviewees responded to question, and many respondents
offered more than one description.

stereotypes. The entire school evaluation system fosters them. The stereotypes respondents provide are not very different from the kinds of evaluations that the school actually uses to describe students. The school records and report cards evaluate students on ability, effort, and cooperation (deportment). The administrators and teachers describe students in euphemisms like talented, motivated, and cooperative. These are the very dimensions that underlie respondents' stereotypes "brains," "grinds," and "momma's kids." The school's evaluation system provides the specific content for the stereotypes that have developed.

Although tracking alone is not enough to create these stereotypes, these stereotypes would not be so broadly applied if there were no tracking system. Tracking provides distinct categories that are highly salient. The students in a particular track are treated quite similarly by school staff (see Chapters 3, 6, and 9). Therefore, although the actual selection is imprecisely implemented and the resulting track placements comprise a diverse collection of students (see Chapter 4), the students in a particular track are perceived and evaluated quite similarly and in stereotypic terms. Tracking provides a highly salient classification onto which the school's evaluations can be projected.

We might wonder whether students take these descriptions seriously. After all, the interview question asked respondents to describe students as members of a track. Such a question cannot detect how readily students apply these stereotypes to particular individuals. Yet there are several reasons for believing that students do take these stereotypes seriously. First, I observed students in different school and nonschool settings, and these stereotypes were often spontaneously mentioned in students' informal conversations to one another (before they knew I was interested in tracking). Second, the patterns of discrimination regarding extracurricular activities and friendship choices point to the stereotypic attitudes found here. Finally, we know from previous research that situations which limit interaction between groups of people tend to foster prejudice and stereotypes, and this is particularly true when the different groups have different statuses (Allport, 1958). Of course, stereotypes are rarely applied to all members of a group; they represent only a tendency to describe group members in a given manner. The stereotypes these respondents offer mean no more and no less than that. They are highly salient, widely held conceptions that students apply to many, although not all, of their peers.

I must note that some respondents do not provide such evaluative descriptions. Yet the students who offer the most negative descriptions are those in the noncollege tracks. Noncollege-track students not only are more likely to use negative evaluations in describing college-track students (e.g., snobs), but they also use negative evaluations in describing students in their own track (e.g., stupid). In contrast, the college-track respondents do not disparage the ability of noncollege-track students. Several college-track respondents noted that some people call noncollege-track students stupid, but these college track respondents explicitly rejected this stereotype and stated their belief that noncollege-track students could succeed in the college track if they were given the chance. Not all students take the negative evaluations seriously; unfortunately, however, the group that is most negatively evaluated gives most credence to these evaluations.[4]

Tracking and Self-Evaluation.   Having seen that tracking molds respondents' evaluations of others, we must wonder how tracking shapes their evaluations of themselves. Researchers often ask people how they view themselves or how high their self-esteem is, but the answers to these queries are difficult to interpret. By definition, the answers are relative, and the standard of comparison is rarely specified. Even if it were specified, the phenomenological issues raised by such a question quickly take one into the realm of the absurd. When one is asked how highly he values himself, he might think, as my friend David Stern has suggested, about economic "value in exchange." One might entertain fantasies like Stephen Benet (1937) about what price to ask for his soul, but he could not even fantasize about selling his "self." Other standards of comparison are equally difficult. Does the self-esteem question ask whether you like yourself better than you like your friend? Or does it ask if you like yourself better than your friend likes himself (although you cannot know that)? Or does it ask if you like yourself better than others like you? The possibilities are numerous, and none have a clear meaning.

My data provide a more relevant and concrete way of looking at students' self-evaluations. As noted in Chapter 6, most students feel they chose the track appropriate for them. Consequently, their perceptions of what they chose (compared with the alternatives foregone) reveal the way they evaluate their school capacities. This is a self-evaluation that is neither abstract nor hypothetical. It represents the way students understand their placement in the school.

Most college-track students (19 of 20) believe that the college tracks offer better education and higher prestige (in the school) than the noncollege tracks and thereby imply that they chose a relatively better position in the school. In addition, they say that they choose to remain in the college track because they feel they are able to do the more demanding work that it requires. Most noncollege-track students (28 of 30) also believe that the college tracks offer better education and higher prestige than the non-college tracks, but this implies that their choice of a noncollege track was a choice of an inferior position in the school. Furthermore, when asked why they chose their track, nearly all noncollege-track students (25 of 30) explicitly state that they chose it because of their own personal shortcomings, either lack of ability or lack of motivation. A student's choice of a noncollege track becomes an admission to himself and to the school at large that he belongs in a lower status position. One student commented:

> Right after I changed to the business track, I felt really ashamed. I avoided my old friends, and I hoped they wouldn't find out. I hid my business track books under my notebook, and I made sure none of my friends were around before I went into a business track classroom.

Another said that after changing to the general track, he felt like he "could never talk to my old friends. I wouldn't have anything in common with them; and, besides, I guess I'm not really smart enough for them to like me." Tracking thus has a clear and important impact on lower-track students' self-evaluations.[5]

Although students might be free to dismiss track stereotypes, and some college-track students actually do, these stereotypes seem to influence the participation, friendship choices, and the self-evaluations of noncollege-track students.

Segregation and Discrimination Based on Inequality of Social Futures. These discoveries lead to a new conception of tracking. Educators define tracking as affecting only pedagogical outcomes, but we have seen that it is also related to students' friendship choices and to their social participation in the school. Furthermore, students also attribute social and personality stereotypes to students in different tracks, and they evaluate themselves and others in terms of these stereotypes.

Although one can never be certain about causality, there are several reasons for inferring that tracking has an influence on adolescent social interaction. The parallels we have seen between formal track structure and the informal adolescent society are extensive and compelling. The academic separation, ranking, and labeling in the track system are accompanied by social separation, social ranking, and social labeling in the informal adolescent society. Furthermore, students themselves perceive that their track placements affect their social interaction and the way they are socially evaluated, and they describe events supporting these contentions. The available evidence implicates tracking as a causal influence on these social attitudes and behaviors.

Of course, this is only a study of a tracked school, and we cannot be sure that these same phenomena would not occur in an untracked school. Thus, if Grayton were not tracked, it is conceivable that differences in academic achievement alone might influence students' participation in school activities, their friendship choices, and the way they are socially evaluated. Although differences in achievement are apt to have some social effects, it is hard to believe that they could have such extreme effects as those we have observed. Failing grades can lead to social stigma, but failing grades are only slowly acquired; they are sometimes contradicted by good grades; and, being not very visible or salient, they become recognized and communicated only imperfectly. In contrast, track position provides a single, highly visible, unambiguous label that instantaneously communicates stigma. Unlike grades, track position directly defines a student's classmates. By defining the group of students with whom one spends his school hours (and, to some extent, his after-school hours), tracking places important practical constraints on a student's friendship choices. Although one must empirically investigate to what extent these social attitudes and behaviors occur in untracked schools, it does not seem likely that an untracked school would lead to such extreme social differences.

Certainly, at Grayton, it is the track structure, and not actual ability, that creates these stereotypes. Although ability is relatively less important than other factors in explaining track placements, and the ability difference between students in different tracks is not clear-cut, respondents tend to characterize college-track students as smart and noncollege-track students as dumb. Though untrue, the school's mythology about selection criteria effectively forms student stereotypes. This makes the stereotyping far more insidious, for the social structure of tracking provides a highly visible distinction onto which the school may project meanings that do not resemble the actual differences among students. As we shall see in the next chapter, this process has important implications for legitimizing tracking and social inequality. Tracking's influence is not the result of actual differences in ability, because we have seen that tracking can actually create stereotypes that are different—and far more extreme—than actual differences among students.

Even more important than these considerations is the unequivocal finding that social segregation and stereotypes have evolved here in the absence of racial or social class differences. Unlike other studies that have investigated the socialization consequences of tracking (Hollingshead, 1949; Schafer and Olexa,

1971), my data were gathered in a socially homogeneous community. Students enter this school with equal social statuses, and, as they acquire different track positions, they also acquire different social statuses and become socialized to different social attitudes, different patterns of social participation, and different self-evaluations. Tracking creates social segregation and invidious social evaluation where neither previously existed.

Furthermore, the effects of tracking are all the more dramatic here because tracking is able to socially stigmatize the noncollege tracks—the tracks leading to working-class futures—within a working-class community! Ironically, and most cruelly, tracking's influence is so independent of community influence that it can stigmatize students for following in their parents' footsteps.

The data of this study provide another perspective on how inequality leads to discrimination. Hollingshead's (1949) classic research argues that differences in social class background lead to social discrimination, and his position has been the main sociological perspective on inequality. My data add another perspective, pointing out that a social hierarchy promoting differences in social class *futures* can lead to the same kinds of social discrimination. Possibly the institutionalized labeling of unequal futures is even more important than unequal backgrounds in creating differential socialization and discrimination.

Track Structure and the Structure of the Adolescent Society.   If tracking actually creates these social influences, then its effects are somewhat at odds with Coleman's portrayal of the adolescent society. His work suggests that the dominant adolescent value system is antischool and that this antischool value system undermines the effectiveness of the school's influence on students. My investigation does not completely contradict Coleman's contention, for it did find a large group of students holding antischool attitudes and engaged in protest and counterculture activities (in 1970). Yet, even within this antischool adolescent society, there are dramatic differences in values, and they are related to (and presumably influenced by) the school's track structure.

Coleman's study did not consider school track structures. If he had, he could have discerned the extent to which they influenced the adolescent society. My study suggests that, although the adolescent society is antagonistic to school, the school's track system influences students' activities, friendship choices, and their evaluations of themselves and others. Thus the track system shapes the very content and structure of the adolescent society. Coleman's causal (independent) variable is related to, and probably dependent on, the school track structure.

Coleman noted the diversity of achievement within the adolescent society, but he chose to deemphasize it.[6] He was alarmed by the degree to which antiacademic attitudes pervaded all groups within the school, even among the high-achieving students. Yet his alarm is warranted only if one considers attitudes to be more important than behavior, for the high-achieving students are doing what school requires, despite their lip service to antischool attitudes. It is as if their academic successes impelled them to pay even greater tribute to antischool attitudes so as not to appear too different from everyone else. Although it is not my purpose to explain these attitudes, I cannot help but note the social functions of a shared adolescent subculture that distracts students' attention from the process of social selection in the school. Whereas most students adulate the star quarterback and the sexy cheerleader, they fail to realize that the college-track students run the student council, the school paper, and most of the other school activities and that these "lackluster" students are the ones bound for upward social mobility. If it were not for the adolescent subculture, the process of social selection would be much more conspicuous and much more offensive to democratic ideals.

The students' own understanding of the adolescent society (which Coleman relies on) overlooks the profound similarities between the adolescent society and the adult society. The adolescent society restricts individuals' access to friendship groups, activities, and leadership positions in a pattern analogous to the social discrimination in adult society. Only the elite are allowed into the best social groups, activities, and leadership positions.

The nonelite are kept out of the best groups and generally prevented from participation in activities and leadership, and, if they do participate, their participation is restricted to lowly service activities or to highly visible, expressive activities (athletics, cheerleading, drama) that offer glamour but little likelihood of upward mobility. Furthermore, the personal characteristics that respondents attribute to students in different track positions are analogous to the social evaluations that Warner's respondents attribute to people in different social class positions. Rather than conflict with the adult society, the adolescent society actually exaggerates social differences among students and thereby recreates and supports the social inequalities in the adult society.[7]

My analysis clearly illustrates a component of the adolescent society other than what Coleman studied. Coleman's research and his Youth Panel Report emphasize a single set of dominant values in the adolescent society and the way these values conflict with adult society. Although it is useful to see the shared characteristics of adolescent society that distinguish it from adult society, this is only a partial perspective. Taken alone, this perspective fed popular fantasies of rampant juvenile delinquency in the early 1960's and of youth revolution in the early 1970's.[8] Neither fantasy materialized, because they were based on an incomplete perspective. Taking another perspective, this analysis has shown that the adolescent society is differentiated into diverse friendship groups, activities, and leadership positions, which allow access based on school track placements and which lead to student evaluations in terms of school criteria. Rather than conflict with school and adult society, the differentiation within the adolescent society is apt to be influenced by the school track system and to reproduce, support, and perpetuate social inequality in adult society.

NOTES

1. One wishes that Coleman had asked students to compare teacher's disapproval with friend's disapproval.

2. The "adjoining" track considered for business was general track, that is, the other noncollege track.

3. Students were asked an open-ended question to avoid suggesting responses to them. The frequencies given are, therefore, lower than one would expect if one had asked direct questions or probes (such as: "Are college-track students smarter?"). The responses not only indicate the *content* of stereotypes but also show that these stereotypes are highly *salient*.

4. This is comparable to the study of Allison Davis and his colleagues (1941), which showed that lower-class respondents tend to be more negatively judgmental in their descriptions than upper-class respondents, even in judging their own class.

5. Although noncollege-track students realize that they have lower status in the school, many do not realize that they will be unable to attend college (see Chapter 6). Several stated that the noncollege tracks were an easy way to get through high school and into college. They felt they would only have to put up with this low status for the few more years of high school. Somehow, college would be much better.

6. Furthermore, the values of the adult society are not as monolithic as Coleman implies. There is no overwhelming consensus in adult society on the value of academic achievement, as Hofstadter's (1964) *Anti-Intellectualism in American Life* suggests. Indeed, my findings suggest that even the teachers and school administrators reflect this ambivalence about academic achievement. Academic ability and achievement are not sufficiently valued to be used as the sole basis for school track placements or even students' grades (Chapter 4). The school considers nonacademic values such as industry and attendance to be more important than academic values. The value differences in the adolescent society are directly parallel to the value differences in the adult society.

7. Of course, I am not saying that tracking perpetuates the original social background positions, since Grayton's college-

track students are upwardly mobile. But tracking does create a system of *social* inequality, over and beyond the inequalities in achievement, IQ, and so forth, that, like societal inequality, creates greater differences than what might be considered functionally necessary or justifiable.

8. Coleman was careful to warn against interpreting his findings to indicate rampant juvenile delinquency, but, in describing the values of the adolescent society, he did not place much emphasis on the variation within the adolescent society or on the effects of schooling in socializing students' values. Thus popular books in the early 1960's often missed Coleman's cautiousness. Coleman is quoted eight times in Hechinger's book *Teenage Tyranny* (1962).

Chapter 9

Socialization for Tournament Selection in School and Society: Theoretical Speculations

Until now, this inquiry has considered selection and socialization separately. This chapter brings the two together, showing the theoretical implications of tournament selection on socialization. It goes beyond the statistical relationships discovered in the previous two chapters and speculates about the social mechanisms that might be involved. Specifically, it generates three different hypotheses: a hypothesis which explains how school selection affects teacher–student interaction and encourages certain kinds of socialization, a hypothesis which explains how schools legitimate track selections and persuade lower-track students to accept the prospect of restricted opportunity, and a hypothesis which explains how society may influence schools and their operation.

Obviously, my data do not allow empirical proof of causal relationships, and so this chapter can only be speculative. Furthermore, the speculations are based on the assumption that my observations are causally related. We must remain aware of the hypothetical nature of the causality assumption, or else we shall fall into the functionalist trap of assuming that all that does exist must exist. This is certainly not my intent; on the contrary, the final chapter will explore how tracking can be reformed. Rather, it is my hope that the causality assumption used in this chapter may be fruitful for contributing hypotheses to guide future research and to improve our understanding of the social processes underlying selection systems.

The hypotheses in this chapter cover a wide realm, and, to explore them, this chapter must relate the sociological analyses of previous chapters to important issues in psychology and economics. The first part of this chapter explores the implications of our findings for psychological research on teacher-student interaction and specifically for research on the effects of teachers' expectations. The second part of this chapter explores the implications of our findings for sociological research on organizational careers and for economic research on education and inequality. This chapter proposes some tentative ideas about the ways that school selection constructs linkages between the micro issues of inequality within a classroom and the broader issues of inequality in society.

Expectancy Effects.   Currently, the most popular explanation of tracking's effects is offered by social psychologists. Rosenthal and Jacobson (1968) demonstrate that, if a teacher is led to expect certain (randomly chosen) students to show marked learning gains, then their expectation will become a self-fulfilling prophecy. The authors infer that expectancy effects may operate through "covert communication" (*ibid.*, p. 160). Good and Brophy (1973) discover an instance of such covert communication in the length of time teachers allow for a student to respond to a question.

Yet I must wonder whether teachers' expectations are either necessary or sufficient to explain the effects of tracking on socialization. Are teachers' expectations *necessary* for tracking's effects to occur? Because Rosenthal and Jacobson wished to conduct a rigorous experiment to study the effects of teachers' expectations, they manipulated only that one factor. Neither their study nor the rest of the tracking literature has investigated other processes through which tracking might operate. I shall consider whether tracking might create other processes that might foster the observed socialization outcomes.

Are teachers' expectations *sufficient* to lead to the socialization consequences I have observed? Rosenthal and Jacobson find that teachers' expectations lead to mean changes in IQ scores, but they do not note the IQ differentiation and homogenization that I have observed. The theory on expectancy effects, like other social labeling theories, might lead us to predict that tracking attaches a particular label to a group of students, and then all students are homogenized to that label (for example, high IQ). Yet my findings do not support such an inference, for I find that college-track students are socialized to differentiated IQs. It is difficult even to imagine why teachers' expectations might differentiate students in the same track or how teachers' expectations would lead to such diverse processes as differentiation and homogenization. One might suspect that there may be some other factor influencing the way these expectations operate in different tracks. In particular, one must wonder if social structural features that social psychologists have not studied might influence the kind of expectations teachers have and the way these expectations influence socialization outcomes.

Does Tracking Create Other Processes?   Although administrators claim that tracking treats all students equally, the tournament structure of tracking is apt to lead quite logically to unequal treatment. If administrators wish to invest the school's educational resources efficiently, then they will logically allocate their resources to students for whom resources can make a difference. The tournament provides no incentive to improve the education of noncollege-track students, for educational differences among them do not make any difference on their fates. Noncollege-track students mostly end up in similar jobs, and the job differences that do occur are not related to differences in their educational achievements (Chapter 5). In contrast, the tournament implies that resources channeled to college-track students will help them compete for positions in college, and their educational achievements will have some bearing on the quality of colleges they attend. Tournament selection is thus likely to lead to unequal treatment of students.

Students report that the school does allocate its educational resources unequally. When asked if students get treated differently in different tracks, most of the interview respondents (34 of 50) report that college-track students receive privileges not granted to noncollege-track students. Furthermore, there is considerable agreement about what those privileges are.

More than half the respondents say that college-track students receive better teachers, better course materials, or richer educational experiences.[1] Students report that only the upper college track is guaranteed of getting all the best teachers, the experimental classes, the field trips to museums and theatres, and the opportunity to meet Senator Kennedy when he visits the school. Lower-college-track students get some of the best teachers and some of the opportunities, but they are not assured of having the best opportunities and resources of the school. The courses offered to the noncollege-track students are often equivalent in subject matter to those for the college track, but these courses use old textbooks that the college tracks had formerly used. Moreover, these courses often omit some aspect of the subject that is a college prerequisite. For example, the science courses for the noncollege tracks omit the laboratory sessions.

Noncollege-track students are not only deprived of privileges

that cost money, they also suffer from other kinds of deprivations. Among the privileges withheld is accurate information
about the track system. Information is an important resource in
any social system, and, as previously noted (Chapter 6), its man-
ipulation in this track system deceives noncollege-track students
about what is happening to them and leads them to make uninformed and undesired "choices."

Privilege in the classroom also comes from teaching differences. Although there seems to be some bias toward guaranteeing
college-track classes better teachers, many of these teachers also
teach noncollege-track classes. But the most important teaching
bias is not in the allocation of teachers but in the way that individual teachers allocate their attention. Teachers report that they
prepare more for college-track than for noncollege-track classes,
and they feel that lower-business and general-track classes are so
undemanding as to require little or no preparation at all. Students report the same phenomenon, noting that some lower-
track teachers assign a workbook exercise every day and then
spend the class period ignoring students and reading the newspaper. Half the respondents say that teachers try harder for the
college-track classes and that the college-track students receive a
better education. Thus, even when the noncollege-track students
get the same teachers as college-track students get, they do not get
as much attention, concern, or effort from their teachers.

Evidently, teachers' attitudes and behaviors sometimes become
transformed from neglect to outright insult, and the track system
literally adds insult to injury. More than a third of the
noncollege-track respondents mention blatant insults directed at
them by teachers and administrators: "Teachers are always telling us how dumb we are." "That teacher doesn't even wait for the
slow kids to answer. She calls on somebody else or answers the
question herself. What's the sense of studying if the teacher
doesn't wait?" One articulate general-track student reported that
he sought academic help from a teacher but was told that he was
not smart enough to learn that material. Several students reported that a lower-track student who asks a guidance counselor
for a change of classes is not only prevented from changing but is

also insulted for being so presumptuous as to make the request.

The reader must feel some skepticism, as I did, at reports of teachers' expressing such degrading insults in front of students. Yet a dozen students report receiving this kind of comment. I heard such comments myself. One of the younger teachers with a more "liberal" reputation told me, "You're wasting your time asking these kids for their opinions. There's not an idea in any of their heads." This comment was not expressed in the privacy of the teacher's room; it was said at a normal volume in a quiet classroom full of students! Students' reports suggest that teachers' expectations are not as subtle as the social psychologists indicate. Good and Brophy's discovery of teachers' waiting time may be subtle to outside researchers, but many general-track students were acutely aware of it.

The teacher's expectations is not the only process that might be operating here. Tournament selection seems to lead to three kinds of inequalities in this school. Economic considerations seem to prompt the tournament to foster inequality of resources (including nonfinancial, but limited, resources such as teachers' attention), and guidance and social control considerations seem to motivate inequalities of information and respect. Furthermore, like teachers' expectations, these three kinds of inequalities might influence socialization.

How Might These Processes Foster Socialization?   I have discovered that tracking seems to foster, not only teacher expectations, but also privileges, deception, and insults, all of which might influence students' socialization. In this section I shall consider how these processes might explain the specific socialization outcomes observed in this study.

Rosenthal and Jacobson might explain my findings of mean changes in IQ and self-evaluation (changes in the latter were inferred rather than shown) in terms of the subtle operation of teachers' expectations, but my observations suggest that this explanation is only a partial answer. Although short-term experiments testing a single artificially introduced variable may have subtle effects, naturally occurring track systems create explicit privileges, blatant deceptions, and gross insults, and these factors are apt to have far greater effects on students' achievements and self-esteem. Teachers' expectations may have important consequences within classrooms, but the kinds of privileges generated by tracking are likely to have a far greater impact in creating differences among classrooms.

My findings on differentiating and homogenizing socialization have not been previously noted in the tracking literature, and they are harder to explain. Rosenthal and Jacobson do not discuss how or why teachers' expectations might have these kinds of outcomes. Indeed, teachers' expectation is such a general process that there is no reason to suppose that it is sufficient to lead to these particular outcomes as opposed to any other outcomes (see next section). But the other processes I have noted—the privileges, deceptions, and insults—may contribute to these particular socialization outcomes.

One might speculate that privileges may stimulate college-track students to perform to capacity and thereby lead them to differentiation in their achievements. On the other hand, being deprived of these privileges, noncollege-track students may consequently receive less intellectual stimulation and feel less involvement. Under such circumstances, they may attempt only to conform to the minimum requirements, and their achievements will be homogenized at that low level.

Although the impact of privilege on educational outcomes is speculative, its effect on social differentiation is obvious. By definition, privilege means a wider choice of options. The many social privileges that college-track students receive constitute a source of social differentiation. A college-track student may participate in many activities (e.g., student council, newspaper, chess club), and he may participate in a diversity of roles within each (see Chapter 8). On the student council, a student may be on the social committee, the curriculum committee, the athletics committee, and so forth. On the school newspaper, he may write news, editorials, sports, or satire. He may be a leader of these activities. Extracurricular activities offer college-track students opportunities to develop a great diversity of skills and to establish individual identities for themselves. If college-track students take advantage of the increased options that accompany their privileged position, they must inevitably become socially differentiated.

In contrast, the restricted participation of noncollege-track students deprives them of this diversity of social skills and assigns them a restricted range of social identities. Noncollege-track students who participate in activities do so largely in service activities, learning functionary roles and acquiring low status (see Chapter 8).[2] Those who do not participate in activities acquire neither skills nor social identities within the institutional structure. Being denied the privilege of full social participation, noncollege-track students acquire homogeneously low social identities. Thus the presence or absence of social privileges leads directly to social differentiation or homogenization.

Insults may also contribute to the homogenization of noncollege-track students. People are often resocialized to accept lower-status positions by what Garfinkel (1956) has called "degradation ceremonies." For example, Goffman points out that new inmates in mental hospitals attempt to deny their inmate status, but hospitals resocialize them to accept this status and conform to this role by subjecting them to various mortifying experiences:

> The new patient finds himself clearly stripped of many of his accustomed affirmations, satisfactions, and defenses, and is subjected to a rather full set of mortifying experiences: restriction of free movement, communal living, diffuse authority of a whole echelon of people, and so on. Here one begins to learn about the limited extent to which a conception of oneself can be sustained (Goffman, 1959, p. 132).

Similarly, the multitude of insults and deprivations that lower-track students experience is apt to undermine their feelings of competence and self-esteem, discourage their interest and involvement in school, and thus homogenize their achievements to a minimally accepted level.[3]

Finally, the deception of noncollege-track students is also likely to make the homogenized socialization effective. Brute coercion is not effective for fostering socialization. People conform when coerced, but they do not internalize their conformity under duress (Kelman, 1961; Inkeles, 1966). Deception is, however, particularly effective at fostering socialization, for it gives people the illusion that they have chosen what they are doing. This is the most subtle and insidious aspect of the track system. Believing that noncollege tracks offer good opportunities, students accept and internalize the role and status that accompany their track position. Only much later do they realize that they were deceived and that they should not have conformed so fully and accepted the negative evaluations so readily. But by then it is too late, for they have already adapted themselves to the restricted role and low status of the noncollege tracks, and this role and status are part of their self-concept. By dispelling reluctance, deception encourages the socialization of noncollege-track students.

Obviously, much of the foregoing is speculation that cannot be verified by data in this study. Yet the relationships outlined here suggest that the privileges, insults, and deception created by tournament selection may lead to the particular forms of student socialization found in this study.

How Might Tournament Selection Influence Expectancy Effects?   Rosenthal and Jacobson give the impression that teachers' expectations inevitably affect student socialization, and yet some failures to replicate their findings (Elashoff and Snow, 1971) suggest that teachers' expectations may sometimes have no effects at all. These failures to replicate have baffled social psychologists and have not been satisfactorily explained (Rosenthal, 1973).

Upon consideration, there is no reason to suppose that altered teachers' expectations will inevitably lead teachers to *act upon* their expectations. If teachers' new expectations are irrelevant to the school's purposes, then these expectations might be ignored. On the other hand, if their new expectations are central to the school's task of selection, then a teacher would feel compelled to act on them. The existence of a track system impels teachers to act upon their expectations.

Rosenthal and Jacobson studied the effects of teachers' expectations in a highly tracked school. The teachers in their study were told that some students would show significant academic gains. This message not only raised teachers' expectations but also indicated that these students were incorrectly placed in a track below their potential. In this situation, teachers must feel compelled to act upon their raised expectations. Indeed, to fail to act upon them would be to permit the continuation of unjust track placements. We might infer that the school's track system was an important factor in inducing teachers to act upon their expectations and to influence student socialization.

In contrast, if Rosenthal and Jacobson's study were replicated in a school that performed no selection among students, where all students were in equivalent classes, then teachers' expectations might not have any impact whatsoever, for teachers would have no reason to act upon their expectations. Similarly, the attribute about which teachers have expectations is important. Rosenthal and Jacobson led teachers to have new expectations about academic achievement, an attribute probably highly valued in that highly tracked school. Yet, I would predict that if the teachers in this school had been led to expect new increases in aesthetic judgment, these new expectations might not have any influence on student socialization (on the assumption that aesthetic judgment was not a selection criterion). The structure and criteria of a school's selection system determine whether or not teachers will act upon new expectations.

The school's selection system may also determine the kinds of expectations and socialization outcomes that occur. Grayton's tournament selection system continually eliminates students from the college tracks. This leads teachers to realize that some students currently in the college tracks will not remain there for long, and the prospect of future eliminations may lead teachers to seek out and discern differences among students and to pick out particular students as candidates for the imminent elimination. Furthermore, a teacher's concern for efficient allocation of his time and attention would lead him to act on his expectations, devoting more attention to students perceived to have good prospects and less attention to students perceived to have poor prospects. Surely, a teacher has little incentive for improving a student's academic skills if he feels that the track system is likely to remove the student from the college track at the end of the year. Tournament selection encourages teachers *to seek out differences* among college-track students, *to respond differently* to them, and thereby to foster differentiating socialization.

On the other hand, tournament selection ignores noncollege-track students, preventing them from moving into college tracks and treating them similarly in job allocations. These structural features lead teachers to *ignore differences* among noncollege-track students, *to respond similarly* to them all, and thereby to foster homogenizing socialization. Thus the structure of the school's selection system may determine the specific expectations that teachers have, whether they act upon their expectations, and the specific kinds of socialization that result.

This structural difference in the opportunities afforded by the college and noncollege tracks creates distinct expectations for students as well as for teachers—what might be considered distinct cultures. The college tracks create a culture of accomplishment, where teachers must expect to discern differences among students, and where students must expect that their accomplishments will help them survive future selections. In contrast, the noncollege tracks create a culture of fatalism, where teachers expect to discern no differences in students' accomplishments, and where students expect that no amount of effort or accomplishment pays off. College-track students learn that social institutions are responsive to their efforts, but noncollege-track students learn that these institutions do not respond.

Social psychologists have not studied structural features of school selection systems in their consideration of expectancy effects and socialization outcomes. My analysis shows that the school's selection structure may determine whether or not teachers have expectations, the kinds of expectations they do have, whether or not they act upon their expectations, the kinds of expectations students acquire, and the kinds of socialization that result. Although my analysis has not proved causal relationships, it has clearly demonstrated that a school's selection structure cannot be ignored.

Legitimizing Tournament Selection by Socialization. Perhaps the most important problem for a selection system is to get people to accept selections. Conceivably, with enough coercion, any selection system can force people into undesired roles, but brute force is inefficient, and social systems try to find ways to legitimate their actions so that participants will accept them. To create legitimacy, tracking presumably must execute a school's selection or socialization functions effectively. A legitimate socialization system would encourage the self-improvement of all students, and yet we have seen that tracking does not do this. A legitimate selection system would execute unambiguous selections based on clearly defined, normatively approved criteria, but we have seen that tracking does not do this. Furthermore, all the potential selection criteria are somewhat unstable and require arbitrary cutoff points, and so it is somewhat doubtful that tracking is able to create a selection system of unquestionable legitimacy.

Yet, as both a selection and a socialization system, tracking is able to create its own justification. Although the track system does not universalistically base selection on students' attitudes or behavior, it is able to socialize students to attitudes and behaviors appropriate to their placements. College-track students become channeled to friendship groups, activities, and leadership positions that encourage appropriate academic skills, motivations, and behaviors, but noncollege-track students are excluded from these groups and positions and enter groups and positions with nonacademic norms. Furthermore, although the track system does not universalistically base selections on IQ, it is able to justify its placements and track changes by socializing IQ increases, decreases, differentiation, and homogenization. The need for legitimacy is most pressing in the case of bright noncollege-track students whose placements are either ambiguous or incorrect. Here the track system is most effective at creating its own legitimacy, for it causes the brightest noncollege-track students to experience the greatest IQ decreases. When a student is placed in the wrong track, socialization processes eliminate the mismatch by making the student fit the track.

The Grayton track system uses a two-stage process to get students to accept their selection to lower-track positions. Chapter 6 showed the first stage, the way Grayton guidance counselors deceive students so that they will choose lower-track placements. As long as students remain ignorant of the track structure, they will accept these positions. But deception is only a short-range strategy. Inevitably, some students will discover the deception and will stop accepting their placements.

The second stage is the process of socializing students to fit into their positions. Deception only sets students up in tracks; it is not enough to keep them there. For that, the track system turns on the socialization processes, which are even more subtle, insidious, and forceful. Students move into lower tracks, unaware of their career prospects and unsuspecting of the socialization processes. Although lower-track schoolwork is easier, it is also boring, and the grade distribution is lower (Chapter 5). Thus downwardly mobile students find schoolwork less intrinsically rewarding, and their interest tends to decrease. They also find that schoolwork does not pay off extrinsically. They learn that the school does not respond to their efforts and academic accomplishments. The school has created a fatalistic culture for the lower-track students, a culture which tells them that social institutions will not respond to them.

In social terms, downwardly mobile students begin to feel uncomfortable with former college-track friends, and they begin to interact with other lower-track students. They adopt lower-track attitudes and behaviors, withdrawing from school activities and "hanging out" on street corners with other lower-track students. As their school interest declines and their activities change, these students become homogenized, resembling other lower-track students.

Deceived choice is only temporarily needed to get students to accept lower-track placements, just as the myth of universalistically applied selection criteria is only temporarily needed. Socialization soon takes over, molding lower-track students to fit their placements and making them incapable of upward mobility. Although selection criteria are not applied universalistically, socialization is universalistic, and lower-track students become homogenized to resemble the official track definition. Although they might not have chosen their track if they had known its implications, before long they must find themselves showing the academic difficulties, diffidence, and disinterest that characterize lower-track students. Socialization manages to change them so that they must resign themselves to accept their lower-track placements.

Coleman's "adolescent subculture" may also play some part in getting students to accept lower-track placements. We have seen that college-track students are concerned with upward mobility and school values, and lower-track students are more concerned with the adolescent-subculture values. Presumably, all students begin with the desire to become successful in life, but the track system limits some students' opportunities for upward mobility. The adolescent subculture provides an alternative value system for students who cannot make it in the upward-mobility value system of the school. This subculture provides these students with an alternative source of status and gratification, diverting their interest away from their original goals. This makes it easier for them to accept the failure that their track position implies. Interestingly, the adolescent subculture places value on consumption (cars, clothes, drugs, sex, and so on), and students lacking mobility opportunities turn to the adolescent subculture in the same way that factory workers lacking mobility opportunities turn to consumption (Chinoy, 1955). The adolescent subculture provides an alternative value system that helps lower-track students accept their track placements and their limited prospects.

Of course, neither socialization nor the adolescent subculture will always be sufficient to persuade students to accept lower-track placements, once students begin to realize their limited prospects for opportunity. No doubt they will feel a great deal of disappointment and resentment at this realization, and, as Stinchcombe (1964) has shown, this may lead them to hedonistic, negativistic, and rebellious attitudes and behaviors. But this realization comes too late to be effective for altering track selections, and students' rebellious responses merely confirm the school's judgment that these students belong in the lower tracks.

This track system, like all selection systems, makes decisions about people's fates that inevitably invite criticism. These decisions could be justified either by making selection procedures meticulously conform to agreed-upon rules or by socializing students to fit their placements. As we have seen, the latter is done here. Tournament selection seems to encourage socialization processes that, in turn, legitimate the selection system itself. Thus, deception is needed only initially to set students in track placements until socialization can take effect. Thereafter, students are soon socialized to fit their placements, and they take on new values, becoming less able and less willing to return to their former track placements. Quite unwittingly, students accept their track placements because tracking has molded them so that they have no alternative.

Societal Support for Tournament Selection.   Of course, tournament selection and its socialization processes do not operate in isolation, and, if we are to understand the processes supporting and underlying them, we must see them in their societal context. Specifically, the tournament model suggests four distinctive attributes of selection: continual selection, one-directional mobility, arbitrary and inappropriate use of selection criteria, and relatively little selection after elimination. Although we have seen that tournament selection is not supported by society's normative ideals, we must inquire whether it may be supported by the actual selection practices in other societal institutions.

We have already noted that tournament selection is maintained in the admissions of Grayton graduates to diverse colleges throughout the state. Students who attempt to go from high school to college are strictly regulated by the constraints of tournament selection. Only college-track students can attend college, and admission is largely based on the same inappropriate and arbitrary criteria as tracking. College admission is just another step in the tournament.

Interestingly, junior colleges were devised with the explicit purpose of offering students a second chance to enter the competition for upward mobility. Yet, despite their contest-mobility purpose, junior colleges have actually become merely a continuation of the tournament. I surveyed junior college admissions officers in the Grayton vicinity and found that the few noncollege-track students who attend junior colleges are restricted to vocational programs in junior colleges and are prevented from transferring to academic programs. Junior colleges in the western states may be less rigid, but the studies that have been done suggest similar tournament selection processes behind the open door policies (see Clark, 1960; Karabel, 1972). Thus even these institutions, explicitly designed to encourage contest mobility, actually operate by tournament selection.

The same finality of selection may occur at later stages of the educational system. Professional and graduate schools sometimes do not allow second chances because they discriminate against older applicants. Many medical schools explicitly state a bias against applicants over the age of 25. More research is needed, but some evidence suggests that the American educational system as a whole resembles tournament selection.

Of course, we have discussed only educational routes to success. Insofar as lower-track students can find alternative routes to success that do not require higher education, the tournament may not apply. Jencks et al. (1972) point out that the educational system is not the only route to success. Yet occupational mobility patterns have some of the attributes of tournament selection. In his review of some of this literature, Glaser (1968, p. 414) notes that "it is usual to find that the higher up on the organizational hierarchy, the more the number of positions in a career pattern." Therefore, people in higher positions are more likely to experience the continual selection of the tournament, and those in lower positions are likely to experience little additional selection. Secondly, although mobility in organizations is said to be flexible and to encourage alternative routes to success, many of the alternative routes are dead-end positions, offering little selection after elimination (Glaser, 1968, pp. 259–306). The real issue in organizational mobility is whether an individual remains on the career ladder to compete for higher positions (e.g., in the tournament) or whether he is shifted to positions outside the career ladder, which, according to the studies reviewed by Glaser, provide no second chances for upward mobility. Finally, Berg cites studies showing that employers in business and government do not base mobility on the explicitly stated criteria (Berg, 1971, p. 89).

The distinction I am making between being "in the tournament" or "excluded from the tournament" is comparable to the dual labor market theory in economics.

> This theory argues that the labor market is divided into a *primary* and a *secondary* market. Jobs in the primary market possess several of the following characteristics: high wages, good working conditions, employment stability, chances of advancement, equity, and due process in the administration of work rules. Jobs in the secondary market, in contrast, tend to have low wages and fringe benefits, poor working conditions, high labor turnover, little chance of advancement, and often arbitrary and capricious supervision (Doeringer and Priore, 1971, p. 165).

This theory emphasizes that workers employed in these different labor markets have different characteristics: skills, work performance, turnover, and so forth. Yet this theory fails to note that the dual labor market is directly supplied by an educational system with a similar dual structure and that this structure may itself help to impart these characteristics to people. The systematic connections between educational selection and the labor market may constitute a fairly unbroken opportunity structure that could socialize people to different kinds of expectations and commitments. One is struck by the similarities between Doeringer and Priore's description of the way workers are treated in the two labor markets and my own description of the way students are treated in the college and noncollege tracks. Both stress the distinctions in rewards, opportunity, equity, and due process.

This theory also ignores structural features that develop over time within the primary labor market (because the theory is largely concerned with describing aggregate differences between the two markets). Although the primary labor market originally offers workers good chances for advancement, it is apt to operate over time like the tournament model, differentiating among its workers and selecting fewer and fewer to retain promotion opportunities. The tournament model may contribute to refining economic theory and analyses.

Another example of this can be seen in Mincer's (1974) econometric analysis of the U.S. Census. Mincer's analysis shows that the variance of workers' incomes increases with experience if the workers are college educated but decreases (or stays the same) if the workers have not attended college.[4] Mincer's findings are important, for like my findings on variance changes in IQ, they thoroughly undermine the traditional assumptions that sociologists and economists use in regression analyses (see Chapter 7, footnote 9). Yet the tournament model permits us to go beyond Mincer's interpretation of his findings. He hypothesizes that variance changes in income are due to (unmeasured) differences in individuals' choices to get more job training (postschool educational investments). He does not consider the possibility that there are systematic and structural reasons for the variance changes or for the differences in additional educational investments which he hypothesizes.

The tournament model brings a new perspective to Mincer's findings. The tournament model says that the job world offers radically better payoffs at successively higher job levels, but the job tournament permits only a portion of each cohort to advance through each successive stage. Consequently, the income variance for each cohort increases over time because the tournament structure permits only a few to rise and leaves many scattered on various lower levels. Of course, this process happens only for those still remaining in the job tournament, and, like the Grayton track tournament, the job tournament admits only those with college credentials. Once a person is eliminated from the tournament in high school or junior college, he is never again permitted to compete in the job tournament for high-income jobs.

Similarly, Mincer's hypothesis that people acquire different amounts of education after leaving formal schooling may be due, not solely to individuals' choices, but also to institutional selection of certain individuals to be tournament contenders. The tournament model suggests that work institutions select individuals to be contenders in the promotion tournament, and the institution then provides these contenders with further education and training (for example, management development, sensitivity training, skills workshops, and formal education programs). The postschool educational investments which Mincer hypothesizes may indeed exist, but, like the unequal investments schools allocate to students, they may be a procedure that the job tournament uses to socialize the elite contenders differentially and to permit further selections among them. Therefore, tournament selection may explain the distribution of income and postschool education in society.[5]

This differentiation in higher positions is also generally recognized by people when they judge the status of occupations. Campbell (as cited in Kahl, 1953, p. 79) finds that people perceive more differentiation in status for upper-level than for lower-level jobs. Rainwater (1974) shows similar findings for income and status. Mincer's, Campbell's, and Rainwater's data do not mean that there are no differences for low-level jobs, but the differ-

ences at these levels are relatively minor. Thus, for those eliminated from the tournament, job selections involve relatively unimportant differences in income and status.

Although we generally assume that the great diversity of colleges, junior colleges, and work organizations offer many alternative routes for opportunity, the available evidence suggests that
all represent a single kind of selection. Furthermore, because
these are the institutions for which the high school is preparing
students, these institutions are likely to influence the selection
process within the high school. Colleges encourage the one-way
mobility of college tracks by providing each high school with a
limited number of slots (which tends to vary only slightly each
year). The diversity in the prestige and quality of colleges encourages high schools to differentiate their college-track students
(and even to sponsor a few for the elite colleges). Furthermore,
colleges do not stipulate explicit criteria or selection rules for
admissions, therefore high schools can use any selection criteria
they wish. In contrast, employers offer high school graduates jobs
with a narrow range of requirements, statuses, and opportunities,
so that the school best prepares noncollege-track students for
such jobs by minimizing the importance of their selections and
evaluations. Thus societal institutions make demands upon
school selection, and the tournament characteristics of societal
institutions are likely to influence the selection system within high
schools.

Linking Schooling to Society.   Bowles and Gintis offer one of the
best explanations for the way society influences socialization in
schools. They contend that "the social relations of schooling are
structured similarly to the social relations of production" (Bowles
and Gintis, 1973). In their view, society is composed of essentially
two kinds of positions, elite and nonelite, and schools identify
students as early as possible as either "future elite" or "future
nonelite" and socialize them to fit into these positions (i.e.,
Turner's sponsored mobility model). The future elite are allowed choices and privileges, which contribute to increases in

their ability and self-esteem, but the future nonelite are coerced and denied privileges, which contribute to decreases in their ability and self-esteem. My findings and speculations support many aspects of this explanation, although I suggest that the actual process may be somewhat more complex than Bowles and Gintis indicate.

Bowles and Gintis are vague about the mechanisms linking school socialization with society's needs (as are most sociologists, see Parsons, 1959). They suggest that elites and their representatives dominate schools by taking positions of power on school boards (see also Useem and Useem, 1974) and by limiting financial resources for lower-class schools. But a school board's centralized policy and finance decisions are rather gross pressures that cannot easily create differential influences within schools (where most differentiation occurs, according to Jencks et al., 1972; see also Stern, 1973).

Bowles and Gintis illuminate various parallels between tracking hierarchies and work hierarchies, but they portray them as static systems, and they do not describe any dynamic mechanisms that might make tracking resemble work hierarchies. According to my analysis, selection may be such a mechanism. Societal selection defines the number and diversity of students to be selected from each track, and the selection criteria used by societal institutions define the relevance of selection criteria for the respective track placements. For example, the number of slots that ordinary colleges and prestige colleges have offered to Grayton's graduates closely matches the number of positions in the upper and lower college tracks, and both figures have remained fairly constant over the last 5 years. Although we do not know whether college admissions practices originally caused the track sizes or vice versa, Grayton's administrators now use this correspondence to justify the sizes of the college tracks. Similarly, colleges' exclusive reliance on track placements—and not ability or effort—for admissions decisions supports the existing track system and poses no challenge to its indifferent use of selection criteria. Thus selection in society supports the selection practices in schools.

In some ways, my analysis leads to outcomes comparable to those described by Bowles and Gintis, but in other ways my analysis departs from theirs. Although I find that there are indeed two groups that may be characterized as the future elite and the future nonelite, these are not entirely distinct groups. Bowles and Gintis assume that selection is stable (like Turner's sponsored mobility model), but I have found that the elite at any particular time are not assured of remaining in that position in the future. Therefore, there are future nonelites among the elites.

Although agreeing with Bowles and Gintis that the future elite are offered privileges and choice, my findings also show that the nonelite are not simply coerced. Radicals, like conservatives, sometimes make the false assumption that choice is the same as liberty, and since radicals believe that society does not permit liberty in such matters, they assume that schools exert coercion. Yet coercion is a crude means of getting people to conform, tending to create resistance and to be ineffective. The school track system, like the societal class system, can be far more effective in convincing low-status people to internalize their conformity by deceiving them into believing that they can still have a second chance for success, while socializing them to make this impossible. This is the real usefulness of the contest-mobility norm: it offers students the illusion of future opportunity—what radicals might call "false consciousness." Rather than deny choice to lower-track students, the track system allows them to make choices based on inadequate or incorrect information. This kind of choice is far more insidious than coercion, for it leaves students more vulnerable to socialization processes that create academic and social obstacles to subsequent track changes, that divert students' attention from opportunity to consumption, and that lead them to accept voluntarily the low status and poor prospects of their track position.

My findings also diverge from the common assumption that tracking affects socialization only through the influence of social class background (implicit in Hollingshead, 1949; Sexton, 1961).

Although social class background clearly influences socialization in the home (Kohn, 1969; Bronfenbrenner, 1970) and teachers' responses to students (Hollingshead, 1949; Rist, 1970), neither of these can explain the selection process or socialization patterns in the socially homogeneous school studied here. Although the combined effects of tracking and social class differences may lead to particularly great differences in socialization outcomes, my findings suggest that removing the social class bias in track placements will not necessarily eliminate these outcomes, for tracking alone can create profound differences in socialization outcomes.

My findings point to increases in ability (and self-esteem) among the future elite and decreases for the nonelite, as Bowles and Gintis predict. Yet my findings also show more complex forms of socialization: differentiating socialization of the elite and homogenizing socialization of the nonelite. As Wheeler has pointed out, these kinds of socialization are also fostered by other institutions in society, and so tracking may prepare students to fit into these subsequent positions. Differentiating college-track students prepares them for positions in elite institutions "which urge recruits to give expression to the different backgrounds and interests which they bring into the organization" (Wheeler, 1966, p. 76). Homogenizing noncollege-track students prepares them for lower-level positions that demand conformity and inter-changeability of workers.

Moreover, my analysis goes beyond Wheeler's observations to suggest structural reasons for differentiating and homogenizing socialization. When the social structure prescribes future selections among individuals in a given position, then that position will tend to foster differentiation along the dimensions of potential selection criteria. In contrast, when the social structure precludes future selections among individuals in a given position, then that position will tend to foster homogenization along the dimensions of potential selection criteria. I have speculated that teachers' expectations, resource differences, insults, and choice may be intervening mechanisms for effecting these socialization outcomes in school track systems. I have noted that similar processes occur in mental hospitals and business organizations, possibly fostering similar kinds of socialization in those settings.

The crucial determinant for socialization is not an individual's social background, but his "social future" as the selection structure defines it. As long as individuals are in the school–society tournament (and can anticipate future selections), the institution must continue recognizing, responding to, and even fostering individual differences in order to continue the selection process. Once individuals are excluded from the tournament (and can anticipate no further selections), the institution can stop recognizing and responding to individual differences and may consider all such individuals as interchangeable and homogeneous.

The latter homogenizing process is consistent with traditional sociological observations about the ways that bureaucracies fail to recognize and respond to individual differences (Weber, 1946), and it is particularly consonant with Lipsky's (1969) description of the teacher's role as a low-level bureaucrat executing a "people-processing" function. Yet this function requires *homogenization only for those positions which offer no further selections* in the bureaucracy. On the other hand, the people-processing function requires *differentiation for those positions which offer future selections* in the bureaucracy. People-processing entails both homogenizing and differentiating socialization, depending on the clients' opportunities in the institution.

Furthermore, this study indicates that the elite are no less the object of people-processing than the nonelite. The differentiating people-processing function operates to the advantage of the future elite, but, in so doing, it also operates *on* them, changing their abilities, motivations, and values, sundering their former friendship ties, and creating stereotypes that are likely to gain credibility as they become more distant from the nonelite. Thus even the elite and the future elite are subject to the people-processing functions in hierarchical social institutions.

My findings for the most part support Bowles and Gintis, and, regrettably, my departures from their position are hardly more flattering to the role of schooling. My analysis deemphasizes the role of the elite in self-consciously controlling the selection process by power, sponsorship, and coercion. Rather, it relies on more subtle and more certain processes. The perpetual operation of tournament selection and uninformed choice creates a systematic process that is not left to the vagaries of human motivation. It fosters stereotypes and socialization processes that legitimate the system, not only to the nonelite, but also to the elite. The tournament is a systematic process that operates independently of elite conspiracies and intentions (for good or ill), that influences the operation of teachers' expectations, and that creates privileges, deceptions, and stereotypes to which all members of the system are subjected.

NOTES

1. Students were asked an open-ended question to avoid suggesting responses to them. The frequencies given are, therefore, lower than one would expect if one had asked direct questions or probes (such as: "Are college track classes given better teachers?"). The responses not only indicate the particular privileges offered but also make it clear that these privileges are highly conspicuous.

2. Star athletes are an exception to this. They acquire glory and prestige during high school, but they find that their status vaporizes after graduation. Athletics offers one of the only sources of status in noncollege tracks, but this status is illusory, and it ill-prepares students for their subsequent fate.

3. Some noncollege-track students reported that some teachers would avoid responding to students' academic questions. In some cases, teachers would poke fun at a noncollege-track student who was "too serious." By referring to such students as "eager beavers" or "wise guys," the teacher discouraged student initiatives in academic areas, both by direct pressures and by mobilizing peer pressures for conformity. Such

teacher behavior was noted only for noncollege-track classes. This lack of respect might contribute to the homogenizing of students' achievements.

4. Mincer's analyses point to a brief initial period of decreasing variances for college-educated cohorts, which are not easy to interpret. They may only be due to random error.

5. I am indebted to David Stern for bringing the Mincer findings to my attention and for helping me think about the implications of the tournament model for economic theory.

Chapter 10

Policy Implications and Proposals

H ow can we improve school selection? Having seen a selection system that has many disturbing features and having reviewed studies indicating that these features may be widespread, we must feel some distress at our discoveries. Furthermore, although this study has helped us see and understand the problems, it has also pointed out that these problems will not be easily solved. Societal ambivalence and normative equivocation have wedged school selection into its present dilemma, and they provide no guidelines for how to extract it from the crossfire of competing values. This chapter tries to rescue school selection from this situation, not by the hopeless task of arguing the superiority of one set of values, but by analyzing the various alternatives. I shall consider several possible policy alternatives and ultimately arrive at one that reconciles competing values and is based on empirically tested consequences. I conclude with some speculations about the implications of this policy for societal selection.

One must wonder at the outset whether it is possible to change school selection without changing society. Is school selection merely a passive reflection of society? If so, then schools are doomed to reproduce and reinforce society's ills, and school reform is a quixotic illusion. My descriptions implied some causality between school and societal selection, but I have no way of knowing which way the causality operates. Chapter 9 assumed societal determinism in order to generate hypotheses, but societal determinism is only an unproved assumption. We cannot, however, let this assumption prevent social action. Indeed, to do so is unscientific, for the only way to learn what can and cannot be done is to attempt social reform.

My research has been particularly well suited to suggesting policy implications. Unlike Jencks's research, which addresses problems too complex to be modified by simple policy manipulations and for which direct solutions are not politically feasible (as he notes, Jencks et al., 1972, p. 263), my research approaches problems at the level of individual schools, where the issue is concrete enough to be understood and manipulated and where direct solutions are feasible. Also unlike Jencks's research, mine is process oriented, describing how selection operates in schools, what the effective mechanisms are (e.g., criteria, guidance, grade weighting), and why the school staff act the way they do (e.g., concern with efficiency, ambivalence, confusion). Hence, this study provides social reformers with ideas about what needs to be changed, where there may be resistance to change, and how to proceed with change.

Furthermore, my research can help dispel much of the mythology and confusion pervading the issue of tracking. We have seen that the school possesses certain myths, which, like mirages in the desert, help the actors proceed by holding out false hopes and mistaken images of reality. Although this mythology functions primarily to mislead students, we might suspect that even the school administrators are taken in. Indeed, educators' confusion may be a large part of the problem of tracking. Educators have failed to recognize the contradiction between their values of opportunity and efficiency, to see the structural similarity between ability grouping and curriculum grouping, to consider the actual school opportunity structure and its implications for selection criteria, or to specify selection criteria or the preconditions for free and informed choice. Research that helps to define the structure and operation of tracking can, therefore, be an important part of reform. Such research can penetrate beyond preconceptions and policy statements and reveal the actual structure, criteria, and consequences of selection, and it can provide the basis for removing confusion, inconsistencies, and injustices.

People who wish to understand and influence educational selection in their schools can themselves conduct research—what I have called "grass-roots research." Although my particular findings may not generalize to all schools, my methods are quite simple and can be easily reproduced. Reproducing this study would not only test the replicability of my findings but would also specify the particular selection issues in a particular school. By clarifying the process of social selection in a school, these procedures might mobilize community concern and suggest policy changes.

This chapter considers several general approaches to reforming Grayton's policies and assesses their adequacy for solving the selection problems we discovered. As we have noted throughout, Grayton's selection problems are likely to be widespread, and the general issues considered here will likely have relevance to other settings. Obviously, different communities will face somewhat different problems and will emphasize different values, so that "grass-roots research" will be important in defining the specific form of policy reached. Yet the underlying principles considered here will be generally applicable for any effort to rethink and reform selection. Let us begin with the simplest and most pragmatic policy reform.

Redefining Guidance Roles to Promote Choice. Perhaps the most disturbing revelation of this study is the lack of free and informed choice. We have seen that the Grayton track policy misrepresents the actual track structure, and the Coleman survey shows that deception about tracking is widespread. We have also seen that guidance counselors offer insufficient or incorrect information to some students in order to influence their choices.

Although shocking, this is not entirely inconsistent with the counselor's role. The school (and society) charge counselors with the responsibility for placing students in proper curricula. If a counselor should allow too many students into college tracks, this would seriously disrupt the school's curriculum offerings, would lead to an overextension of college-track resources, and would result in far too many college-track students' being excluded from college (following the school's assumption that colleges maintain the same admission rates from the school).[1] The school requires that counselors shape students' track choices in a way that preserves the track system as it has been. In other words, the counselor's primary responsibility is the school's (perceived) needs, rather than the students' needs.

Of course, the counselor's role is officially defined quite differently. Officially, the counselor is supposed to provide students with advice and information so that students can make choices promoting their own interests. Students sometimes want a counselor to help them make appropriate choices, and so, conceivably, the officially defined counselor role could satisfy students' needs. Yet the counselor provided by the school cannot meet students' needs, for his primary responsibility is to the predefined interests of the school. Whenever the students' interests conflict with the school's interests, the counselor will be unable to serve both, and he is more likely to serve the school.

A simple partial remedy of this situation is to increase the amount of information that is disseminated to parents and students. Grayton is not unusual in the limited amount of information that it disseminates. Cicourel and Kitsuse (1963) point out that even the affluent suburban high school they studied did not give parents much information about school selection. The simple tables that I constructed on the track opportunity structure (Chapters 3 and 5) would be extremely helpful to parents and students in understanding the choices they must make. Publishing relevant information would prevent counselors from using deceptive information to influence students' choices.

A second and more thorough response to this role conflict is to delegate the counselor's two roles to two separate persons. One person would serve the school's interests, and the other would serve the students' interests. This would create an adversary model of guidance similar to the adversary process in law and would provide an institutional protection for students' interests. It would also offer a means of implementing the recent Supreme Court ruling about students' rights in cases of school dismissal.

But small pragmatic solutions such as these are insufficient for dealing with the problem of selection. The deceptive guidance practice in Grayton is a small symptom of the fundamental inconsistency between the contest norm and the tournament structure. These reforms do not address the fundamental value conflict between open opportunity and efficient early selection. Consequently, these reforms do not offer a program for planned change, and they will either be unsuccessfully implemented, or they will lead to unforeseen changes. On the one hand, the forces maintaining the contest norm and the tournament structure might prevent the students' counselor from having any impact, since he would be the single impediment to the school's functioning as it had. School officials would treat the students' counselor just as they had treated students, denying him information or preventing him from effective protest. On the other hand, the students' counselor would be given sufficient staff and authority to be effective in minimizing deception, but the result would be the school's inability to fill noncollege-track positions and the downfall of the tournament structure. If this happened, the school would have no way to handle the conflict between opportunity and early selection.

These reforms may lead to some improvement. But it is not
enough for a community to decide to eliminate deception; it must
also reach a decision on how it will deal with the fundamental
issue of opportunity versus early selection. Any attempt at selection reform must directly confront these issues.

Implementing an Ideal Tournament.   We have discovered that the
Grayton track system implements what may be called a tournament selection system. The rule for tournament selection has
been simply defined—when you win, you win only the right to go
on to the next round; when you lose, you lose forever. Although
the permanent selections created by a tournament are offensive to
our values of open opportunity, they might be justified as promoting educational efficiency. Efficiency is an important value in
our society, and it is one of the presumed advantages of tracking
(in both the ability grouping and curriculum grouping literature;
see Chapter 1). Furthermore, efficiency of educational selection
was one of the primary purposes for Binet's developing the IQ
test and for the continued development of the test in the United
States (see Marks, 1972). The widespread use of tracking and IQ
tests in American schools suggests that efficiency is an important
value in education and that tournament selection might be a
tenable ideal for selection in society.

Yet the question is whether early permanent selection is actually efficient. The entire vocational education movement is premised on the assumption that separating vocationally oriented
students into specialized classes will help them get better jobs.
The business track in Grayton fully embodies this assumption; it
even separates students in all their courses for as long as six years
so that their curriculum can be highly specific and directed toward vocational goals. But all of this assumes that the world of
work will respond to the school's track categories, and my data
suggest that the work world is not very responsive to vocational
preparation programs.

This conclusion is confirmed in a nationwide survey of more

than 5000 graduates of 25 high schools in diverse communities (Kaufman et al., 1967). This study concludes that, although there were small differences in the job types (manufacturing vs. clerical) obtained by students from different tracks,

> graduates from all three curricula (college, vocational, and general) tended to earn about the same amount of money, to remain on jobs for about the same length of time, to leave jobs for much the same reasons, and to have about the same levels of job satisfaction. . . . The vocational graduates clearly thought that they had been better prepared for their jobs than did the academic or general graduates. These attitudes of the respondents, however, were not confirmed by their direct supervisors who rated the preparation of students provided by all three curricula about the same (*ibid.*, p. 124).

In part these conclusions may reflect failures of vocational programs to provide good preparation.[2] Probably far more important, however, is the fact that the job world offers all high school graduates approximately the same kinds of jobs. Early permanent selection can hardly be efficient if it leads all noncollege students to similar jobs.

The pedagogical model of tracking contends that tracking is also efficient for the development of academic achievement. Again, the assumption is that the separation of students into homogeneous groups (based on past achievement) leads to teaching efficiencies. This assumption has been repeatedly tested by numerous studies of achievement gains and losses; but, as we have noted, the general conclusion to be drawn from this research is that tracking is not very consistent in its pedagogical consequences. On the single criterion of achievement, tracking seems to produce gains for some at the expense of losses for others, and these gains do not always occur. This literature does not highly recommend tracking's efficiency.

Of course, this literature does present some cases where there are gains, and so one might be tempted to conclude that tracking is sometimes efficient. From a methodological standpoint, however, such an inference is unwarranted, for we would expect a certain number of achievement gains from all those studies just on the basis of chance. Yet, more importantly, achievement gains are not the sole grounds for assessing tracking. Educational research has emphasized achievement gains and losses as if they were the only value at stake. But the real issue is how tracking balances the value of efficiency with the value of opportunity; that is, to what extent do pedagogical gains outweigh the costs of restricted opportunity? Conceivably, deciding the tradeoffs between these two values could be difficult, but in fact, virtually no tracking studies find large mean achievement gains. My own study of a highly rigid track system finds some large increases, but the mean increase for the college track as a whole are rather minor and are easily offset by the costs to noncollege-track students in terms of restricted opportunity (and IQ decreases). When put in this perspective, early permanent selection is not sufficiently efficient in producing achievement gains for college-track students to justify its costs in terms of restricted opportunity for the other students.

My results not only question the outcomes of early permanent selection but also give us reason to doubt whether it can be meritocratic. Meritocratic early permanent selection assumes that a stable selection criterion exists and that school staff are willing to use such a criterion. Yet my analysis casts doubt on both assumptions. I find that IQ test scores are not always very stable. Furthermore, my analysis suggests that track placements are based on the least stable school record indicators rather than on the relatively stable ability tests.

IQ is the best candidate for a meritocratic selection criterion, and indeed it was devised with that in mind. The stability of IQ scores was of particular concern to the developers of the IQ test (Cronbach, 1949). Yet we have seen that it is not very stable in Grayton. Although there are several possible reasons for the instability of IQ scores in this setting (see Chapter 4, footnote 5), the inescapable fact is that they cannot be depended on to be stable in all settings. Indeed, my analysis shows that IQ scores change in ways that support the school selection structure and thereby compound selection errors (Chapter 7). Therefore, even

IQ, the test specially designed for early meritocratic selections, cannot be relied upon to be suitable for such selections.

Furthermore, the stability of IQ scores is irrelevant if test scores are not used, and the Grayton track system does not seem to place much reliance on them. A closer look at the guidance counselors' feelings about IQ tests makes these findings understandable. Although Grayton's counselors express considerable confidence in IQ tests, they are dismayed when the test scores conflict with their personal feelings about a student, and, in these cases, they tend to discount the test scores. In discussing which students have college potential, counselors praise some low-IQ students, whom they consider personable and industrious, and they disparage some high-IQ students, whom they consider lazy. They also distinguish between test performances and teachers' judgments of students' abilities, considering the latter to be better ability indicators than test scores. The objectivity and detachment of standardized tests make them valuable in selecting unknown students to enter a new school or college (the original purpose of Binet's test and the current use of the College Board exams). Grayton may rely heavily on these tests in tracking new students from other school systems. Yet in making selections *within* a school, counselors often personally know students and their previous teachers, and the very objectivity and detachment of standardized tests make them less immediate and less compelling than subjective criteria.

Thus the problem with a tournament selection system has less to do with ideal values than with realities. Although the presumed efficiencies of early selection are not entirely discrepant with some of our values, these presumed efficiencies are not supported by research. Early selection does not lead to efficient job allocation nor to significant achievement gains. Furthermore, my research suggests that school staff may be unwilling to use stable objective criteria for selections within a school.

Implementing a Contest Track System.   Molding a track system to fit the contest-mobility norm would seem to be a desirable policy, combining some of the (presumed) pedagogical advantages of tracking with the opportunity advantages of the contest norm. This might be implemented as a track system that creates separate tracks of homogeneous classes but allows track changes every year. Yet we must wonder whether a track system can permit opportunity. We have seen Grayton's claim of a contest track system to be untrue, but need it be so? Can a track system allow upward mobility? To answer this question, we must consider two important issues. First, can schools offer preparation for unequal futures without compromising equal opportunity? Second, can schools offer separate, but equal, education? These are fundamental issues underlying educational selection, and my analyses of Grayton can help us address them.

Can schools offer preparation for unequal futures without compromising equal opportunity? Equal opportunity is supposed to offer equal inputs but to produce unequal outcomes. Tracking's problem arises because it connects outcomes with inputs and thereby makes students' unequal futures influence the education that school offers them. A lower track prepares students for less academically demanding jobs; and, in so doing, it deprives them of the academic preparation they would need for upward mobility in the track system. Thus, even if a lower-track student is able to move into a harder track, his upward change is likely to fail because he will find it difficult to catch up with what he has previously missed. The Grayton track system actually did allow a few noncollege-track students to switch to college tracks, but these students found that they had missed important skills and concepts, and nearly all of them switched back to noncollege tracks. Thus, even when this system permits upward track change, the nature of tracking prevents such change from being successful. If a school is to offer all students equal opportunity for college track, then it must offer them a minimum amount of college preparation sufficient for success in the college track.

However, even this minimum amount of equality may not be enough. Can schools offer separate, but equal, education? Track-

ing raises this question in a much broader context than racial
segregation (see *Brown* v. *Board of Education of Topeka*, 1954).
Tocqueville warned that America's ideology of equality might
preclude all kinds of separation and differences. Can schools
offer diversity without fostering inequality? The rhetoric of the
vocational education movement proposes that school curricula
can be separate but equal, and, at least in terms of initial financial
outlays, vocational education programs have not been
shortchanged. Yet in the half century since this movement began,
most communities have witnessed the deterioration and stigmati-
zation of their vocational education programs. And even when
the financial investments to vocational education continue to be
high, the social investments may be low. We have seen that
Grayton's noncollege-track students receive less teacher attention, outright deception and insults, fewer opportunities for
school participation, and social discrimination among peers.
Even within a socially homogeneous community, track distinctions have created inequalities of social status. Even within a
working-class community, the noncollege tracks, which prepare
students for working-class jobs, confer low status. Thus curriculum diversity *creates status differences where such differences had
not previously existed and confers stigma to working-class job prospects in
a working-class community.*

This process might occur regardless of how flexible a track
system might initially be. Even if a track system provides all
students with a sufficient minimum amount of college preparation to permit upward mobility, any vocational courses that are
offered to only some students can still become socially stigmatized. The dynamic would be the same as in Grayton. The
vocational courses would still be stigmatized as marginal to the
school's academic values and as preparing students for low-status
positions. As long as some students take somewhat more of the
socially valued college prep courses and others take somewhat
more of the socially stigmatized vocational courses, inequalities of
social status can be preserved in a school, and they can lead to

differences in education, guidance, school participation, informal interaction, and self-concept, and they can create the informal barriers to upward mobility.

Within an institution which values academic training and a society which values college education, tracking is likely to create educational and status distinctions that may militate against upward mobility. My study shows that, even in a homogeneous working-class community, a track system can create status differences and stigmatize working-class preparation and thereby create barriers to upward mobility that did not exist previously.

Of course, although I have argued that this is likely to happen and I have shown that it can happen, I have not shown that it will inevitably happen. It may be possible to set up a flexible track system permitting upward mobility, although this has never been demonstrated. Furthermore, even if one did exist, the preceding analysis suggests that such a track system will always face the risk of creating status distinctions that ossify placements and undermine the contest ideal. The logic of this analysis means that a contest track system always contains the risk of becoming a tournament system.

An Empirical Resolution.   A pure contest system in schools might be considered irresponsible. Schools are supposed to select students and offer them different kinds of preparation. A pure contest system—which delays selections until after school ends—would execute neither of these functions. It would treat all students exactly the same, offering them the best education possible.

It is illuminating to consider what would happen differently if this pure contest system were implemented in high schools. Selections after graduation would not be altered much. Colleges would still execute their selections, based on much the same criteria as at present, except that college selections would be less contaminated by track influences that do not reflect ability or effort. The job world would continue to execute its "selections," placing applicants in fairly similar jobs with little reliance on school criteria. If schools stopped performing the selective function tomorrow, society would carry on making selections without noticing the difference.

It is not selections as such that society needs from schools but, rather, the different kinds of preparation that schools execute after selections have been made.[3] Students going to college require different preparation than those going to work. This is where a pure contest system is thought to be dysfunctional and to provide a disservice to students. If all students are given college preparation throughout high school in order to preserve their opportunity to attend college, then one might think that students not selected for college will lack any preparation for the job world and will presumably be at a disadvantage in securing a job.

Yet we have seen that, even in the rigid and highly segregated Grayton track system, the noncollege tracks offer a minimum amount of vocational preparation. Students in the business tracks get virtually the same kinds of jobs as those in general tracks. Even college-track graduates who do not attend college get these same jobs. The only vocational skill that distinguishes the jobs of Grayton's graduates is typing, and surely, this does not require six years of specialized and segregated preparation in all of one's courses.

I am now in a position to propose an ideal track policy that reconciles the competing values of opportunity and efficiency and permits the timing of selection to be empirically tested. I propose that *all selection distinctions be delayed until further postponement can be empirically shown to be detrimental to student preparation.* This leads to a pure contest system that ends only when specialized preparation becomes necessary. My analysis of Grayton suggests that the specialized training necessary to prepare students for their current job distinctions would take very little time. A single course in typing in the final year of school might accomplish the same results as Grayton's six years of tracking. Even a vocational program superior to Grayton's might be done in two years, as evidenced by private business schools that provide job training in two years or less. Furthermore, the time of selection could be further delayed by inserting a few vocational courses in the early curriculum taken by all students. In any case, rather than define the precise time for selection for all schools a priori, one can empirically study what kinds of specialized preparation and job distinctions are accomplished by a particular track system and then assess whether selection can be postponed further without hurting that preparation.

The essence of this policy is to place *the burden of proof on those who propose selection distinctions.* This policy assumes that the fundamental purposes of schools are to provide education and opportunity, and any deviation from these purposes, to provide efficient selection or job preparation, must be empirically justified.

This policy provides the degree of equality needed to encourage equal opportunity. It delays and minimizes educational differences so that all students receive adequate preparation for college as long as possible. It delays and minimizes status differences in order to minimize the risks of social stigma as long as possible. It also maximizes opportunities for individual growth and development. Psychological research suggests that early learning and socialization have more penetrating and more far-reaching impact than later learning; therefore, delayed selection leads to less extensive inequalities' being socialized into students. Furthermore, psychological research has shown that the rate of personality and intellectual development, like the rate of physical development, varies, so that delayed selection allows greater opportunity for detecting late-developed talent. This policy provides the greatest opportunity for late-developed talent to be recognized, for selections to have the least damaging impact on personality and intellectual development, and for mistaken selections to be reversed.

A policy of minimizing selections is the only one that can be justified by existing selection criteria. My analysis of school criteria concludes that only a track system that delays and minimizes track distinctions can be justified. We have seen that the Grayton school record indicators provide no completely stable and validated measure. Even the ability indicators, which are relatively stable, are not sufficiently stable to justify distinctions that might damage students' life chances. Thus, properties of potential selection criteria require that schools delay and minimize selections as much as possible.

A policy of delaying and minimizing selections is also the only one that can be justified by choice. Students' choices cannot have much meaning at the age of 13, nor can a student make important decisions about his life career while he is still discovering his capabilities and interests and before he has learned what the world of work has to offer. Even if students' choices are informed and advised by student-oriented counselors, counselors' advice will be based on imperfect predictions about students' potential capacities, and incorrect predictions can have great costs for the student.

Furthermore, the forced "choice" between academic and vocational preparations creates particularly high risks and costs for those who are most eligible for upward mobility, that is bright working and lower-class students. Their choice of academic preparation precludes vocational courses that might provide them with some job security if college attendance became unfeasible (or with a source of part-time income to finance college). On the other hand, the choice of vocational preparation minimizes risk at the cost of precluding college attendance. Early selection for specific preparation can actually lead to inefficient outcomes if it compels bright students to choose job security in place of continued education.

Contrary to the axiom of conservative political philosophy, choice is not always the same as liberty, for sometimes people prefer to retain all options. The requirement to make a choice does not permit the freedom to postpone the choice. Only a structure that delays and minimizes selections—allowing at least a minimum amount of both academic and vocational preparation—can preserve students' options for choice.

Finally, this policy creates a system that publicly reveals the way a school balances the values of opportunity and efficiency. This policy demands that any and all distinctions and selections must be empirically justified on the grounds of efficiency, by using the same kinds of analyses I have used in analyzing Grayton. This means that the community will have specific information about what they are gaining and losing by permitting any particular kind of distinction, and it prevents the deceptions practiced in Grayton.

Philosophical Objections: Homogeneity and Coercion. One can imagine several kinds of objections to a policy of minimized distinctions, and, by dealing with each, one can better refine and specify the implications of this policy. The first and most general objections might be called philosophical, because they stem from philosophical concerns about undesirable consequences of egalitarian policies. Philosophers have worried that egalitarian policies might lead to uniformity. Tocqueville warned that the American effort to prevent inequality might lead to a monotonous homogeneity. Must a policy of minimized distinctions produce a homogeneous environment and highly similar individuals?

Certainly a school that minimizes distinctions need not be monotonously homogeneous. On the contrary, although such a school might offer all students a single curriculum, that curriculum would have to provide both academic and vocational preparation. That curriculum would be more heterogeneous than the curriculum offered to a student in a single track of a track system. Furthermore, an untracked curriculum would not make all students homogeneous, for students differ in their interests and abilities, and a single highly differentiated curriculum would permit different students to develop different interests and abilities.

This can be contrasted with what we have seen in Grayton. Grayton's track system produces a heterogeneous curriculum overall, but students do not have access to this heterogeneity. They can be in only one track, and within each track, they are limited to a rigid and homogeneous curriculum. Students passing through either curriculum might find it monotonous in its specialization. In addition, my results show that the noncollege tracks actually operate to homogenize students who pass through these tracks.

A somewhat related philosophical concern argues that egalitarian policies attempt to eradicate existing individual differences and are thus coercive. This concern is evident in conservative ideologies (see the novels of Ayn Rand) and even in liberal essays (see John Gardner, 1961). Yet rather than compel equality, egalitarian policies can be enacted to prevent societies from compelling or institutionalizing inequalities.

The track policy proposed here provides all students with the same education and the same general status. This does not eliminate inequalities. Students will differentially absorb education and will acquire different grades and statuses from their performances. Obviously, a student who sometimes gets failing grades will tend to become known and stigmatized in ways that may affect expectations, friendships, self-esteem, and even his future career. Yet the process is a slow and not very certain one, depending on the gradual accumulation of bad grades, the imperfect communication of these invisible marks, the contradiction of these marks by occasional good marks, and the different responses to these marks by peers. In contrast, track position provides a single, highly visible, unambiguous label that instantaneously communicates stigma and directly defines one's classmates and likely career chances. The track policy proposed here does not preclude individual differences or consequent evaluations, but it does discourage the school from seeking out, amplifying, reifying, or systematizing these differences into official labels that have predefined institutional implications.

Although a policy of minimized distinctions need not be coercive, it may be somewhat restrictive in the choices it offers. The danger with electives is that they may become selective, recreating the separation, status differences, and educational inequality of a track system. This does not mean that all students must take identical courses, but it is essential that all students take equivalent courses (i.e., courses that are interchangeable for preparing one for subsequent selections). Although this policy limits the possibilities for choice, it is far less limiting of choice than the Grayton track policy, which makes a single language elective be highly influential for one's entire high school career. A policy of minimized distinctions requires that all distinctions have minimal implications for later selections.

Of course, all of this is easier to describe than to implement. There is always the possibility that any system allowing choice will create a selective system. This could be detected by a monitoring system using procedures similar to those used in this research. One would look out for systematic patterns where particular choices feed into subsequent selections. Or one would look for guidance counselors' statements that attempt to persuade some students to choose one of the supposedly "equivalent" courses. Conceivably, students' own preferences, unabetted by school influences, will create selection distinctions, perhaps through social class differences in family values (see Kohn, 1969), in which case, one must face a difficult decision between equal opportunity and free choice.

Yet we are hardly at that point now in Grayton or in other track systems. It is not individual choice but school policies that prevent equal opportunity in track systems, and alleviating this problem does not require policies that restrict individual choices but rather policies that restrict coercive track systems. Minimizing and delaying selections will actually increase the heterogeneity in a student's curriculum and will decrease the coercion that limits his options.

Pedagogical Objections: Teaching Difficulty. Many teachers contend that it is easier to teach classes that are homogeneous because the students' needs are more similar. On the face of it, this argument is compelling, and it is presumptuous for a researcher to tell a teacher what constitutes ease of teaching. Yet there are reasons to doubt this argument.

First, although there can be no doubt that it is easier to treat all students similarly, this may not be appropriate for teaching "homogeneous" classes. Classes that are homogeneous in achievement (or ability, industry, or some other aspects) may not be homogeneous in learning style or learning needs. Students can score in the top third of an achievement test by being good at vocabulary but not at grammar, or vice versa. Some students learn best through abstract presentations, and others learn best from concrete presentations. We do not know the best way to group students to make them homogeneous in learning needs. Therefore, it is likely that any "homogeneous" grouping that we might create would still require teachers to treat students differently if they are truly to respond to students' learning needs.

Second, my findings of IQ differentiation within the college track suggest that teachers may actually respond differently to students in homogeneous classes. Presumably, it would not be any more difficult to respond differently to students in heterogeneous classes.

Third, it is hard to know how much emphasis to place on the argument of teaching ease, if improving teaching ease leads to costs for students' opportunities. We have seen that tracking may make teaching easier because teachers feel no need to expend effort on lower-track students (whose opportunities cannot be altered by educational improvements). If this is the source of teaching ease, then it is a reason for abolishing tracking and making teaching more difficult. Yet, even if tracking leads to legitimate teaching ease, then it is still hard to balance the benefits for teachers with the costs to students.

Actually, the teaching ease argument is unprovable in the abstract, for teaching ease will depend, not only on classroom composition, but also on teachers' experiences, techniques, and so on. Ease is a conservative argument, for it is always easier to continue doing what one has been doing than to make changes. Of course, this argument might work in the other direction once the teacher has become accustomed to teaching heterogeneous classes. Furthermore, some teaching techniques are better suited to heterogeneous classes than others, and the teacher's particular repertoire of techniques may influence teaching ease. Thus, although traditional lecturing might not be as easy in heterogeneous classes, some teachers who use open-classroom techniques say that it is no harder to teach heterogeneous than homogeneous classes. These teachers encourage students to help other students in small groups and thereby free themselves from many routine demands. This sort of teaching technique is ideally suited to heterogeneous classes, where some students are in a position to be helpful to others.[4]

Once again, I would urge an empirical test of the argument. Initially, it should be tested by teachers who volunteer to experiment. They should be provided with adequate resources and training in appropriate teaching techniques. If the test proves successful for the first volunteers, then there will be more volunteers. It is important that teachers' commitment be voluntary so that they harbor no resentments to the program. Clear commitment by the school system can facilitate teachers' commitment, particularly if the school system's commitment is reflected in incentives, resources, and prestige.

Of course, any attempt to reform tracking must consider the possibility that teaching ease and student opportunity may conflict. A tracking experiment must define in advance to what extent teaching ease might be sacrificed to students' opportunity and how the school would compensate teachers if sacrifice were judged necessary. The opposite decision—sacrificing student opportunity to teaching ease—is unpleasant to consider, and it is hard to imagine how students might be compensated for lost career opportunities.

The experiment demands sustained commitment for several years before the outcome is certain. Certainly, the time of transition would be difficult, for change is always difficult, and the school would have to continue its commitment to the teaching staff during this period. Furthermore, no one can be certain how the experiment would turn out. But the experiment is warranted, for the alternative is a track system that has enormous costs for its students. Certainly, the costs of not experimenting are great.

Societal Obstacles.   Until now, we have considered school reform without regarding societal influences. I have suggested that school reform can be effective for minimizing selections and their implications, and yet, we must expect that, until societal selection is changed, reform will be an uphill battle. Students must ultimately enter society and be subjected to social selection. School reform can do nothing to change this inevitability; school reform would appear as only a delaying action, and one must wonder if it is worth the effort. My analyses suggest several reasons why a delaying action is worthwhile.

First, delay allows time for students to show a greater range of achievements, to reveal late developed talents, to stabilize their development, and thus to produce more and better data upon which selection can be based. Hence, delayed selection allows students more opportunity and allows the school to make better selections.

Second, delaying selection postpones the consequences of selection, which exaggerate differences, create privileges, and segregate, evaluate, stereotype, and socialize students. By postponing these consequences of selection, selection reform leaves lower-track students less damaged so that they are personally more capable of subsequent upward mobility if they are offered a second chance, and they are happier about themselves in any case. As Sennett and Cobb (1972) point out, many of the psychological injuries of social class are perpetrated by invidious comparisons in schools, and delaying selection to the end of school diminishes such injuries.

Finally, delaying selection may even encourage greater equality in society. Just as societal forces can influence the dynamics in schools, so schools can affect societal structures. By postponing selection and its consequences, selection reform limits the amount of time available for socializing students to fit into different tracks. This means that lower-track students are likely to leave school with better education, fewer years of separation, less stigmatized status, and better self-concepts. Consequently, they will be better qualified to hold good jobs and be more confident of their strengths. They will be less accepting of boring, ill-paid, dead-end jobs.

Thus, I disagree with Jencks's conclusion that school reforms cannot influence social inequality. Although my data agree with his findings that the empirical correspondence between school evaluations (IQ, grades, and so on) and placements is a myth, tracking uses this myth to foster stereotypes and different socialization patterns and thereby justify inequalities in students' careers. This myth encourages teachers in school track systems to seek out, amplify, and institutionalize student differences, making students suitable for, and accepting of, societal inequalities. School reform can undercut these socialization processes by delaying selection and thereby encourage greater societal equality.

Obviously, school must continue to be related to society's needs to some extent. My proposal to delay selection so that all students receive college preparation should also include some vocational education courses for all students. A few vocational courses will offer all students some knowledge about the manual job world and some security that they have practical skills if they were financially unable to continue in school. In addition, because all students would be enrolled, vocational courses would be less likely to be stigmatized, and they might be better courses. Finally, these courses would further delay the time when selection would be necessary.

In recent years, the President's Youth Panel Report (Coleman et al., 1973) and several high-level federal officials [notably, Wirtz (1973) and Marland (1973)] have been concerned about high job turnover, job dissatisfaction, and unemployment among youth, and they have recommended that education be reformed so that it be better related to the needs of the work world. Some of their proposals have suggested increasing the vocational specialization in schools to improve students' job preparation.

Given the results of previous vocational programs (see Kaufman et al., 1967), I cannot be very optimistic that such programs will improve youth's job preparation. But my results suggest that such programs may be effective in socializing youth to have lower expectations, lower self-esteem, greater homogeneity, and more experience with boring, unrewarding, low-opportunity positions. School selection can be effective at socializing students, but a free society that aspires to encourage open opportunity must be wary of using this power.

I would suggest that, rather than impose early selection systems on the school to make school fit the work world, these reformers might seek to change the selection process within the work world. Rather than try to prepare youth for boring, ill-paid, dead-end jobs, they might attempt to change the jobs: allowing job enlargement, greater income equality, more participation in decision making by all employees, and greater opportunity for advancement. Such job changes would be tantamount to extending our school reforms into society, minimizing the consequences of selections in the workplace.

Ultimately, reforming job selection is the best way to bolster selection reform in the schools. Minimizing the consequences of job selections would reduce both the importance of college credentials and the need for deception, manipulated choice, and homogenized socialization. Some inequality and selection may be needed in society (see Dahrendorf, 1968), but there is no need for the degree of inequality that our society now has. Minimizing societal inequality and selections would relieve school of some of the pressures for selection and relieve school selections of the burden of finality.

Although I would agree with Jencks's recommendations for equalizing societal positions, these reforms will not come easily or soon. In the meantime, school reform can make a difference on the careers of students and on the legitimacy of societal inequality. Given the unpromising immediate prospects for large-scale societal change, grass-roots research and school reform provide a more tractable place to begin.

NOTES

1. This assumption is mentioned by school staff in other schools besides Grayton. School administrators and counselors seem to treat the relative size of the various tracks as an immutable fact.

2. Given the rapid rate of technological change in industry, schools cannot afford to supply the latest equipment for training. Therefore, vocational programs often train students in obsolete skills.

3. I discuss the third function of tracking—socialization—later in the chapter.

4. This arrangement offers benefits not only to those who are helped but also to the helpers. To teach others, students will have to clarify the material in their own minds to explain it to those they are helping, as many new teachers have observed. This point was called to my attention by two of my own teachers, Irving and Dorothy Rosenbaum.

Bibliography

Alexander, Karl L. and Bruce K. Eckland. 1974. "Sex Differences in the Educational Attainment Process." *American Sociological Review,* Vol. 39, No. 5, October, pp. 668–682.

Allport, Gordon. 1958. *The Nature of Prejudice.* New York: Doubleday, Anchor.

Balow, I. H. 1964. "The Effects of Homogeneous Grouping in Seventh-Grade Arithmetic." *Arithmetic Teacher,* Vol. 11, No. 3, pp. 186–191.

Benet, Stephen Vincent. 1937. *The Devil and Daniel Webster.* New York: Farrar and Rinehart.

Berg, Ivar. 1971. *Education And Jobs: The Great Training Robbery.* Boston: Beacon.

Billett, R. O. 1932. *The Administration And Supervision of Homogeneous Groupings.* Columbus: Ohio State University.

Blalock, Hubert M. 1960. *Social Statistics.* New York: McGraw–Hill.

Bloom, Benjamin. 1964. *Stability And Change in Human Characteristics.* New York: Wiley.

Boocock, Sarane. 1972. *An Introduction to the Sociology of Learning.* Boston: Houghton–Mifflin.

Borg, W. R. 1966. *Ability Grouping in the Public Schools*, 2nd edition. Madison, Wisconsin: Dembar Educational Research Service.

Bowles, Samuel. 1972. "Schooling and Inequality from Generation to Generation." *Journal of Political Economics*, May–June.

Bowles, Samuel and Herbert Gintis. 1973. "IQ in the U.S. Class Structure." *Social Policy*, Vol. 3, No. 4 and 5.

Bronfenbrenner, Urie. 1970. *Two Worlds of Childhood—U.S. and U.S.S.R.* New York: Simon and Schuster.

Brown v. *Board of Education of Topeka*. 1954. 347 U.S., p. 483.

Callahan, Raymond E. 1962. *Education and the Cult of Efficiency*. Chicago: The University of Chicago Press.

Carden, Maren Lockwood. 1969. *Oneida*. Baltimore: Johns Hopkins.

Chinoy, Ely. 1955. *Automobile Workers and the American Dream*. New York: Random.

Cicourel, A. V. and J. Kitsuse. 1963. *The Educational Decision-Makers*. Indianapolis: Bobbs–Merrill.

Clark, B. 1960. "The 'Cooling-Out' Function in Higher Education." In *Education, Economy, and Society*. A. H. Halsey et al., Eds. New York: Free Press. Pp. 513–526.

Clasby, M. et al. 1973. *Laws, Tests, and Schooling*. Syracuse, New York: Syracuse University.

Clausen, J. A., Ed. 1968. *Socialization and Society*. Boston: Little, Brown and Co.

Cohen, David K. and Marvin Lazerson. 1972. "Education and the Corporate Order." *Socialist Revolution*, Vol. 3, March–April.

Coleman, James. 1961. *The Adolescent Society*. New York: Free Press.

Coleman, James et al. 1966. *Equality of Educational Opportunity*. Washington: U.S. Government Printing Office.

Coleman, James et al. 1973. *Youth: Transition to Adulthood*. Washington: U.S. Government Printing Office.

Conant, James B. 1967. *The Comprehensive High School*. New York: McGraw–Hill.

Cronbach, Lee. 1949. *Essentials of Psychological Testing*. New York: Harper and Row.

Dahrendorf, R. 1968. "On the Origin of Inequality among Men." In *Essays in the Theory of Society*. R. Dahrendorf, Ed. Palo Alto, California: Stanford University Press. Pp. 151–178.

Davis, Allison, et al. 1941. *Deep South: A Social-Anthropological Study of Caste and Class*. Chicago: University of Chicago Press.

Davis, Allison. 1952. *Social Class Influences upon Learning*. The Inglis Lecture, 1948, Cambridge, Massachusetts: Harvard University Press.

Davis, Kingsley and Wilbert E. Moore. 1945. "Some Principles of Stratification." In *Class, Status and Power*. Reinhard Bendix and Seymour Martin Lipset, Eds. New York: The Free Press. Pp. 47–53.

Doeringer, Peter B. and Michael J. Piore. 1971. *Internal Labor Markets and Manpower Analysis*. Lexington, Massachusetts: Heath Lexington Books.

Elashoff, J. D. and R. E. Snow. 1971. *Pygmalion Reconsidered.* Worthington, Ohio: Charles A. Jones.

Eysenck, H. J. 1971. *The IQ Argument.* New York: Library Press.

Findley, W. and M. Bryan. 1971. *Ability Grouping: 1970.* Center for Educational Improvement, Athens, Georgia: University of Georgia.

Freeman, Richard B. 1975. "Overinvestment in College Training?" *Journal of Human Resources,* Vol. 10, No. 3, Summer, pp. 287–311.

Gardner, John W. 1961. *Excellence, Can We Be Equal and Excellent Too?* New York: Harper.

Garfinkel, Harold. 1956. "Conditions of Successful Degradation Ceremonies." *The American Journal of Sociology,* Vol. 61, March, pp. 420–424.

Glaser, Barney. 1968. *Organizational Careers.* Chicago: Aldine.

Glaser, B. and A. Strauss. 1967. *The Discovery of Grounded Theory.* Chicago: Aldine.

Goffman, Erving. 1959. "The Moral Career of the Mental Patient." *Psychiatry,* Vol. 22, May, pp. 123–131.

Good, T. L. and J. E. Brophy. 1973. *Looking in Classrooms.* New York: Harper and Row.

Goodlad, John. 1960. "Classroom Organization." In *Encyclopedia of Educational Research,* 3rd edition. Chester Harris, Ed. New York: Macmillan. Pp. 221–225.

Griggs v. Duke Power Co. 1971. 401 U.S. 424.

Hall, Em. 1970. "On the Road to Educational Failure: A Lawyer's Guide to Tracking." *Inequality in Education,* No. 5. Harvard Center for Law and Education.

Hansen, Carl F. 1964. *The Four Track Curriculum.* Englewood Cliffs, New Jersey: Prentice–Hall.

Heathers, Glen. 1969. "Grouping." In *Encyclopedia of Educational Research,* 4th edition. R. L. Ebel, Ed. New York: Macmillan, Pp. 559–570.

Hechinger, Grace and Fred Hechinger. 1962. *Teenage Tyranny.* New York: Crest.

Herrnstein, Richard. 1971. "IQ." *The Atlantic Monthly.* September, 1971, pp. 43–64.

Heyns, Barbara. 1971. "Curriculum Assignment and Tracking Policies in Forty-eight Urban Public High Schools." Unpublished Ph.D. dissertation. University of Chicago.

Heyns, Barbara. 1974. "Social Selection and Stratification within Schools." *American Journal of Sociology,* Vol. 79, No. 6, pp. 1434–1451.

Hobson v. Hansen. 1967. 269 F. Supp. 401 (D.D.C.).

Hofstadter, Richard. 1962. *Anti-Intellectualism in American Life.* New York: Vintage.

Hollingshead, A. B. 1949. *Elmtown's Youth.* New York: Wiley.

Illich, Ivan. 1970. *Deschooling Society.* New York: Harper and Row.

Inkeles, Alex. 1966. *What Is Sociology?* Englewood Cliffs, New Jersey: Prentice-–Hall.

Jencks, Christopher. 1972. "The Quality of the Data." In *On Equality of Educational*

Opportunity. F. Mosteller and D. P. Moynihan, Eds. New York: Vintage.

Jencks, Christopher et al. 1972. *Inequality: A Reassessment of the Effect of Family and Schooling in America*. New York: Basic.

Kahl, Joseph. 1953. *The American Class Structure*. New York: Holt.

Karabel, Jerome. 1972. "Community Colleges and Social Stratification." *Harvard Educational Review*, Vol. 42, pp. 521–562.

Katz, Michael. 1971. *Class, Bureaucracy, and Schools*. New York: Praeger.

Kaufman, Jacob K. et al. 1967. *The Role of the Secondary Schools in the Preparation of Youth for Employment*. University Park, Pennsylvania: Institute for Research on Human Resources, The Pennsylvania State University.

Kelman, Herbert C. 1961. "Processes of Opinion Change." *Public Opinion Quarterly*, Vol. 25, pp. 57–58.

Kirp, David L. 1973. "Schools as Sorters: The Constitutional and Policy Implications of Student Classification." *University of Pennsylvania Law Review*, Vol. 121, No. 4, April.

Kohn, M. L. 1969. *Class and Conformity*. Homewood, Illinois: Dorsey.

Light, Richard J., and Paul V. Smith. 1971. "Accumulating Evidence: Procedures for Resolving Contradictions among Different Research Studies." *Harvard Educational Review*, Vol. 41, No. 4, November, pp. 429–471.

Lipset, S. M. and R. Bendix. 1959. *Social Mobility in Industrial Society*. Berkeley: University of California Press.

Lipsky, Michael. 1969. "Toward a Theory of Street-Level Bureaucracy." Paper presented at the annual meetings of the American Political Science Association, September, New York.

Low-Beer, John. 1975. "Perspectives on Social Inequality." *Yale Law Journal*, Vol. 84, No. 7, pp. 1591–1602.

Marks, Russell. 1972. *Testers, Trackers, and Trustees*. Ph.D. dissertation (unpublished). University of Illinois.

Marland, Sidney P., Jr. 1973. "Career Education: Off the Drawing Board." *School Review*, Vol. 82, No. 1, November, pp. 57–66.

McKinley, Donald G. 1964. *Social Class and Family Life*. New York: Free Press.

Mercer, Jane. 1973. *Labeling the Mentally Retarded*. Berkeley: University of California.

Mincer, Jacob. 1974. *Schooling, Experience, and Earnings*. New York: National Bureau of Economic Research.

Morland, J. Kenneth. 1964. "Kent Revisited: Blue Collar Aspirations and Achievements." In *Blue Collar World*. Arthur B. Shostak and William Gomberg, Eds. Englewood Cliffs, New Jersey: Prentice–Hall. Pp. 134–143.

Mosteller, F. and D. P. Moynihan. (Eds.) 1972. *On Equality of Educational Opportunity*. New York: Vintage.

NEA Research Division. 1968. *Ability Grouping*. Research Summary 1968–73. Washington: NEA.

Otto, Henry J. 1941. "Elementary Education—II, Organization and Administration." In *Encyclopedia of Educational Research*, W. S. Monroe, Ed., 1st edition. New York: Macmillan. Pp. 428–446.

Otto, Henry. 1950. "Classification of Pupils." *Encyclopedia of Educational Research*, 2nd edition. Walter S. Monroe, Ed. New York: Macmillan, pp. 376–378.

Parsons, Talcott. 1959. "The School Class as a Social System: Some of Its Functions in American Society." *Harvard Educational Review*, Vol. 29, Fall, pp. 297–318.

Passow, A. H. 1962. "The Maze of Research on Ability Grouping." *Educational Forum*, Vol. 26, pp. 281–288.

Piven, F. F. and R. Cloward, 1971. *Regulating the Poor: The Functions of Public Welfare*. New York: Random House.

Rainwater, Lee. 1974. *What Money Buys: Inequality and the Social Meanings of Income*. New York: Basic.

Rist, Ray. 1970. "Student Social Class and Teacher Expectations: The Self-Fulfilling Prophecy in Ghetto Education." *Harvard Educational Review*, Vol. 40, pp. 411–451.

Rosenbaum, James E. 1973. *"School Stratification and Student Careers."* Unpublished Ph.D. dissertation, Harvard University.

Rosenbaum, James E. 1975. "The Stratification of Socialization Processes." *American Sociological Review*, Vol. 40, No. 1, February.

Rosenthal, Robert. 1973. "On the Social Psychology of the Self-fulfilling Prophecy: Further Evidence for Pygmalion Effects and Their Mediating Mechanisms." New York: MSS Modular Publication.

Rosenthal, R. and L. Jacobson. 1968. *Pygmalion in the Classroom*. New York: Holt.

Rothstein, Robert. 1971. "Down the Up Staircase: Tracking in Schools." Chicago: New University Conference.

Rubington, Earl and M. S. Weinberg. 1968. *Deviance/The Interactionist Perspective*. New York: Macmillan.

Schafer, W. E. and C. Olexa. 1971. *Tracking and Opportunity*. Scranton, Pennsylvania: Chandler.

Scheff, T. J. 1966. "Typification in the Diagnostic Practices of Rehabilitation Agencies." In *Sociology and Rehabilitation*. Marvin B. Sussman, Ed. Cleveland: American Sociological Association.

Schur, Edwin M. 1971. *Labeling Deviant Behavior*. New York: Harper and Row.

Selltiz, Claire et al. 1962. *Research Methods in Social Relations*. New York: Holt, Rinehart and Winston.

Sennett, Richard and John Cobb. 1972. *Hidden Injuries of Class*. New York: Random.

Sewell, William H. and Vimal P. Shah. 1967. "Socioeconomic Status, Intelligence, and the Attainment of Higher Education." *Sociology of Education*, Vol. 40, Winter, pp. 1–23.

Sewell, William H., et al. 1970. "The Educational and Early Occupational Status Attainment Process: Replication and Revision." *American Sociological Review* Vol. 35, December, pp. 1014–1027.

Smuck v. Hobson. 1969. 408 F.2d 175 (D.C.Cir.).

Sexton, Patricia. 1961. *Education and Income*. New York: Viking.

Sørenson, Aage Bottger. 1970. "Organizational Differentiation of Students and

Educational Opportunity." *Sociology of Education,* Vol. 43, Fall, pp. 355–376.

Stacey, Judith et al. 1974. *And Jill Came Tumbling After.* New York: Dell.

Stern, David. 1973. "Some Speculations on School Finance and a More Egalitarian Society." *Education and Urban Society,* February, pp. 223–238.

Stinchcombe, Arthur. 1964. *Rebellion in a High School.* Chicago: Quandrangle.

Sudnow, D. 1965. "Normal Crimes: Sociological Features of the Penal Code." *Social Problems,* Vol. 12, Winter, pp. 255–270.

Tanner, Daniel. 1965. *Schools for Youth.* New York: Macmillan.

Tatsuoka, Maurice M. 1971. *Multivariate Analyses: Techniques for Educational and Psychological Research.* New York: Wiley.

Thomas, R. M. and S. M. Thomas. 1965. *Individual Differences in the Classroom.* New York: McKay.

Tocqueville, Alexis. 1945. *Democracy in America,* New York: Random.

Turner, Ralph. 1960. "Modes of Social Ascent through Education: Sponsored and Contest Mobility." *American Sociological Review,* Vol. 25, pp. 855–867.

U.S. Office of Education. 1962. *What High School Pupils Study.* Washington: U.S. Government Printing Office.

Useem, Elizabeth and Michael Useem. 1974. *The Education Establishment.* Englewood Cliffs, New Jersey: Prentice–Hall.

Warner, W. Lloyd et al. 1946. *Who Shall Be Educated?* London: Kegan Paul.

Warner, W. Lloyd, et al. 1949. *Democracy in Jonesville.* New York: Harper.

Warner, W. Lloyd and Paul S. Lunt. 1941. *The Social Life of a Modern Community.* New Haven, Connecticut: Yale University Press.

Weber, Max. 1958. *The Protestant Ethic and the Spirit of Capitalism,* New York: Scribners.

Weber, Max. 1946. *Wirtschaft und Gesellschaft.* Part III, Chapter 6, pp. 650–678 in *From Max Weber.* Trans. by H. H. Gerth and C. W. Mills, Eds. New York: Oxford. Pp. 196–266.

Wechsler, D. 1958. *The Measurement and Appraisal of Adult Intelligence.* Baltimore: Williams and Wilks.

Wheeler, Stanton. 1966. "The Structure of Formally Organized Socialization Settings." In *Socialization after Childhood.* Orville Brim and S. Wheeler, Eds. New York: Wiley. Pp. 51–113.

Wilson, Alan. 1959. "Residential Segregation of Social Classes and Aspirations of High School Boys." *American Sociological Review.* Vol. 24, pp. 836–845.

Winer, B. J. 1962. *Statistical Principles in Experimental Design.* New York: McGraw–Hill.

Wirtz, Willard. 1973. "Education and a National Manpower Policy." *School Review,* Vol. 82, No. 1, November, pp. 79–90.

Wolfle, Dael. 1960. "Educational Opportunity, Measured Intelligence, and Social Background." In *Education, Economy, and Society.* A. H. Halsey et al., eds. New York: Free Press. Pp. 216–240.

Yates, Alfred. Ed. 1966. *Grouping in Education.* New York: Wiley.

Young, Michael. 1958. *The Rise of the Meritocracy.* Baltimore: Penguin.